Unbreakable Resolve

Triumphant Stories of 3 True Gentlemen

ISBN: 978-0-9997125-0-4

Cover design by: Michael Mooney

Contents

Your Free Gift

To show our appreciation we've put together a free gift for you.

It is a compilation of sayings we wrote while in prison and since our releases. We hope that among these words you will find comfort, inspiration and the empowerment you seek.

http://unbreakableresolvebook.com/freegift

Just visit the link above to download it now.

Thanks!

Robert Jones, Daniel Rideau, Jerome Morgan

Human progress is neither automatic nor inevitable.... Every step toward the goal of justice requires sacrifice, suffering, and struggle; the tireless exertions and passionate concern of dedicated individuals.

Martin Luther King, Jr.

Dedication

I'd like to personally dedicate this book to my brothers whom lost their lives to senseless street violence: Pierre, Denerreal, Lee and, now, Chris. Y'all rest well.

—Robert Jones

This book is dedicated to my two children, Daniele J Rideau and Daniel J Brickley who suffered the most from my absence. I love you infinitely and thank you for loving me despite my heap of flaws.

—Daniel Rideau

I dedicate this book to the memory of my older brother, Harry Anthony Morgan. He was murdered in November 2003, at the age of 30, after being released from Angola Prison in 2000. Also, to my brother's daughter, my niece, Kenisha Davis, and my brother's granddaughter, Ta'Liyah. To my son, and my two nephews, let this book be a guidepost in your darkest hour. Always know that the light is within you!

—Jerome Morgan

Preface

The society of the urban youth is in a dormant state of suffrage, bondage, and death. Too often, it seems that there are no outlets for youths to prosper, let alone maintain. They are tossed in these cycles of society; inadequate education systems, inadequate health/mental health systems, inadequate housing or living conditions, a long list of deficiencies, which compiles into a life of feeling inadequate. If only at some point in time in a youths' life can the misfortunes be turned around to the fulfillment of dreams. Far too often so many youth, "slip or fall through the cracks," without the proper encouragement they need and deserve. Or, a view to see another outlook on life, unlike today when the cracks sometime get so wide that they are unavoidable.

In response to a WVUE 8 New Orleans Fox news segment, the Founders of Free-Dem Foundation decided to write a book of their own personal trials and struggles; to offer an alternative to a mother who feels her son "slipped through the cracks" thus leading to him losing his life. With the testimony of Founder, Mr. Robert Jones, a clear path is displayed to how the lack of adequate education and living wages can create a necessity to do wrong in order to maintain. From Founder,

Mr. Daniel Rideau, his story of the essence of family, single motherhood, and overall survival are the exponential points. The final story, that of Mr. Jerome Morgan, brings broken families, and fitting-in to the forefront.

Independently each of the Free-Dem Foundation founders individual stories is powerful and heartfelt, but, collectively, they are the lessons needed to help "seal the cracks." The state of the urban youth in the United States remains an issue debated in many different 'schools of thought.' Media outlets, family, friends, and most of all, historical writings, influence the perceptions formed by individuals on behavior of urban youth. Evidence shows a clear connection between the ways subject matters are written and how the same subject matters are perceived. Another influence of perception is presentation, how a subject matter is presented to the public holds bearing on the overall perception of that subject matter. The stories presented in this book show that perception is not always correct.

—Derrick Martin, mutual friend of Robert, Jerome and Daniel

Tell the Truth

The first time I saw him, he was handcuffed. I sat with approximately 20 students at a hearing. After the formal part of the hearing, the judge called me up and encouraged me to continue bringing young people to the courthouse. Our students at the Center High School program had been working on the Jerome Morgan case for over a year. The hearing eventually led to Jerome's release.

In 2017, after 20 years of incarceration and over five years of fighting for exoneration after being released, Jerome Morgan, along with Daniel Rideau and Robert Jones, tell their own stories of being caught-up in America's criminal justice system.

The stories that these men tell are important. Why? Because what happened to them reflects what happens to literally millions and millions of people entrapped in the normal, day-to-day operation of the American mainstream—Away of life that advertises freedom and justice for all, while daily dealing mass incarceration and systemic oppression to many.

A major part of being human is the search for meaning in one's life. Who am I? How did I get in the condition I'm in? Why me? For many people—particularly those of us who are so-called minorities—the quest for meaning is tied up with fighting against "is-ims and schizims," i.e. the American way. Black people were stolen from Africa and imported into America as raw labor. We were forced to work 24/7. Slavery and Jim Crow required a police force to control us and a system of laws to justify our oppression and to govern our submission.

Although we have a long history of resistance, the story of how we survived and developed has not been extensively documented at a mass level. Our lives are at the core of American history but our voices and specific conditions are not fully acknowledged in the public school curriculum. We may have black history celebrations in major cities and be seen on television shows but we don't teach the specifics of how we came to be who we are.

The two places that are filled with young people are the public school class room and the state prison system. Even though the classroom directly feeds the prison cell, rarely do those two places connect with each other.

Students at the Center (SAC) is an independent writing program that works in the high schools of New Orleans. A SAC staff member was working as a private investigator and connected Jerome Morgan's case with our in-school work. Jerome's fight for exoneration became part of the SAC daily curriculum. Our students studied about his case in the classroom, exchanged letters with him while he was incarcerated, and attended his courtroom hearings.

SAC believed in education for liberation rather than simply for mainstream socialization. We wanted to create students who would think for themselves and who understood that their real social conditions should be a major part of their classroom curriculum. Although SAC was not the norm of high school education, SAC was a vital connection between the classroom and community. Our students were literally the brothers and sisters of the incarcerated.

Even though the mainstream doesn't usually deal with the specific conditions of injustice, we believed that public education should deal with public problems. And we are not alone. In major urban areas as well as on isolated reservations, in rural communities and in college towns, groups of people are organizing to resist. Educators and activists are working together with inmates and the formerly convicted to address a system of injustice.

Indeed, in America we have a long history of resistance to oppression. Every day more and more of us are not only speaking out, we are also writing down our stories. Unbreakable Resolve is the New Orleans response to the national phenomenon of repression by the mainstream.

Three men document their stories. They speak to and for all of us. They write about the human desire to be free. They directly address the social reality of life in modern America.

Each, in their own way, add to the literature of liberation. They celebrate life and liberty. They represent the spirit of freedom and justice that beats in the hearts of all humans everywhere.

Hear their stories. Read their words. Their individual truths shall help set all of us free.

—Kalamu ya Salaam, Educator, New Orleans public schools

Robert's Story

As I sit here contemplating on what to write or say to the youth and people I am trying to reach. It's only fair that I tell you what happened to me.

I grew up in New Orleans, Louisiana a poor black boy raised in a single parent household just like the average young black boy in America. I am the eldest of five other siblings. My mother, Lois Marie Jones (a super woman), was left to raise all her six children after my father was killed, and after my younger brother and sister's father left her. She did not have much education to get better jobs, so she had to settle for odd jobs here and there. For the most part, my mother practically made all ends meet from selling all sorts of homemade candies and other junk foods from her back-apartment door in the Desire housing projects of New Orleans, Louisiana.

Everybody in the neighborhood used to call my mother the "Candy Lady." It's funny now as I remember, she did credit before we understood what credit is. I remember people used to come and get items, but couldn't pay until they got their monthly government check or paycheck from working. My mom also used her talent in sewing to the fullest. She sold laced socks for little girls to other parents in the area. In short, my mother was a real hustler as we call it today.

I learned a lot from my mother. She instilled values and principles in me that carry me through life, even to this day. She used to tell me, "Boy, you have to work hard at whatever you want in this life. You have to act like your life depends on it." Unknowingly, those pearls of wisdom would be the very words I relied on to fight for my freedom years later.

Looking in from the outside one would have thought it was easy for me growing up because my mother was doing okay with her side hustle. This later became her only source of income after she stopped working to take care of us. In addition, she had welfare checks and food stamps coming every month. I recently found out, however, that the government will cut a welfare recipient's check and food stamps if they make over a certain amount of money at a job. Make me wonder if that's why my mother stopped working.

I remember those rough years growing up poor. There were times my mother had to under-pay bills in order to keep clothing on our backs and food on the table, mainly, because foods stamps were not enough to feed six growing kids. I also can recall the many nights I would eavesdrop by my mother's bedroom door. She would be crying out to God saying, "God, please help me to raise these kids and make them better than me." It breaks my heart even to this day because I can still hear her sad voice pleading to God for help.

In 1984, my mother starting dating a new guy, Jack Samson (not his real name). Jack was a good person and treated my mother right for the most part. He was a self-employed type of guy who knew how to fix any and everything. He did for us as much as he could when he and my mother got serious. At first, I didn't take to him well because I felt in my mind after my father was killed that I was the man of the house. In my opinion, I think many other young boys in this position feel or felt the same way about a "new dad."

I assumed the role as a man by trying to help my mother out with things around the house. My younger brother and I developed a hustler mentality at an early age. We use to go to all the grocery stores near our neighborhood to help shoppers carry their bags to their cars for a fee. It was going well, but too many other young black boys was doing the very same thing, so we took our hustle to the car washes. We washed cars for a fee—today it is called "detailing." Nevertheless, the extra money was good. We were proud to give our mother some money to help around the house. At first, we got chastised for not getting my mother's permission to go to these places, but somehow, we convinced her that it was clean hustles and all the kids around the neighborhood were doing the same thing. She allowed us to only do it on the weekends after completing our chores, but we often did it on weekdays as well, unbeknownst to her. It was decent money that we made, but still wasn't enough to satisfy our materialistic desires for the latest fashion trends and high priced sneakers. Trust me, it is not a good feeling seeing other kids your age with the things that you want and can't get. The peer pressure was serious because those kids would make fun of you and cause embarrassment. As a result, I couldn't get what I wanted from my mother, so I started to pay close attention to the "Big Timers," another name for a high-level drug dealer. Big Timers had other guys, some even younger than me selling his drugs, all while he rode around in a luxury car, draped in diamonds and playing on all the pretty ladies in the neighborhood.

Although I watched the dealers, it took years before I even attempted to try the game—Primarily, because my mother, aunts and older cousins used to help get things for us. When those options ran dry, I gave selling drugs a try. My brother and I sold marijuana roll ups to people we did not know, nor did they know us. We didn't want our mother to find out. I was maybe 14 and my brother was 13 years old. We were doing well, helping out around the house with food and clothing for our brothers and sisters. Of course, my mother thought the money was coming from our car washing on the weekends. However, one day someone obviously saw us selling drugs and told my mother and older cousins. My cousins were drug dealers themselves. When my mother found out, she flew into our shared room in a rage. She found all our saved one dollar bills in a sock under the mattress along with some weed. She took it all and flushed it, even the money. Then she made us throw away every item of clothing that she had not bought. Afterwards she and our older cousins beat us like we were grown men.

We stopped for a while, but eventually started back selling drugs in another way. We were working as a watch out boys for big time drug shops. We managed to do this at night when my mother would go to sleep. We use to sneak out the house sometimes through the front door and come back in by climbing threw our room window. We use to get paid all the one dollar bills from that night. Sometimes it use to be two hundred dollars or more. This went on for a while until one day our cousin showed up at the drug house. Funny thing was, it was his drug shop and we were working for him and neither of us knew it. When he saw that we were going to do it no matter what he took us under his wing. My mother was devastated and crushed. She beat us over and over, and even threatened to send us to jail. I continued to go to school to calm my mother, but still managed to sell drugs on the side. She refused to take any money from me and swore She was going to put me out on the streets.

This news was also shocking to my aunts and other family members who knew I had been raised better. I remember growing up around real community leaders and caring older people. I used to go to the community center to learn different things about life, but mainly how to box. I was encouraged to follow in my father's footsteps as a professional boxer. I seemed to learn faster than most of the other kids because unbeknownst to the trainers, my dad used to teach me at home at an early age. I attended and participated in a few events, but became discouraged in becoming a boxer because of all the hard training. I smile as I write this now, because the same hard training I used to complain about ended up being the very required skill set that helped me defend myself in fights against bigger and older guys growing up in prison years later. Those experiences tell me that you never know why you have to do certain things in life.

In 1987, the year, in my opinion, when sports started to really highlight black athletes or should I say the merchandise that bore those athletes' names. I mean if you didn't own a pair of Jordan's, Ewing's, or Danny Ainge sneakers, you might as well have stayed inside. We growing teens, used to practically beg our parents to get these types of sneakers. We all were like addicts for this stuff. This is something I still see in today's teens, but worse. It's totally insane to see how consumers, mainly young and older black men and boys as well as the parents of younger boys, camp out in front of stores waiting on the arrival of the latest Jordan's. Other popular athlete's sneakers have a similar effect, but not like Jordan's. Nevertheless, those athletes inspired us to want to play sports. We used to mimic all of their moves on each other, playing in the neighborhood gyms or parks—specifically, Samsun Park. Samsun Park was what I called the park that produced a lot of good athletes from the downtown area. One Hall-of-Famer comes to mind—The great Marshall Faulk. He is a childhood friend of mine that used to stand out from everyone. I remember watching him play in NFL games on television years later. I would be smiling in my heart, literally because some of the moves I saw him put on defense players, were some of the same moves that he used to do at Samson Park and Carver High School or in friendly neighborhood games.

Overall, my point is that back then I knew the impact of how community centers, leaders, parks and positive things of that nature can have a productive effect on the lives of growing youth. I also knew how the negative influences in the neighborhood could have a negative impact on the youth, primarily because they influenced me. In spite of my mother's objections and disappointments of my actions, I continued to sell drugs. She eventually put me and my younger brother out of her house to protect the rest of her children. I and many other people couldn't understand her logic, but now, being a wiser man, I do understand. She told me if I couldn't abide by her rules, then it was time for me to get my own house. Then I could live by my own rules. It was a courageous and hurtful move for her, but as my life developed it was necessary because it made me who I am today.

My mother moved miles away from the Desire housing projects in 1987. My brother and I went found an apartment to rent on a relative's property, a few blocks away from my mother's house. I soon had to learn about the responsibilities of a house, such as bills and other things, although I never personally had to pay the bills to the agencies. Crazy, because I had to get adults or pay adults to do those things for me. Of course, it wasn't a problem because money was coming in fast from the new crack game sales. I laugh now reflecting back because I had a car and all without driver's license the first. It's unbelievable because I was only about fifteen years old and my brother was fourteen years old. Eventually we both dropped out of school because it was getting in the way of us making more money. We would buy gifts and clothing for our other brothers and sisters to help take the burden off our mother. She used to refuse it at first, but after our relentless efforts of sneaking the gifts and clothing in the house she just gave in. I used to explain to her that our way of life was not her fault, but our own choices. Eventually, I started sleeping at her house more after being searched at the door for drugs and illegal things of the sorts that she did not want in her house or around her other children.

Life was moving fast for me. I somehow ran into a big connect as we called it. A connect was foreigners or non-blacks who brought tons of cocaine into the country to give to mostly blacks to sell to their communities. I would soon learn that these so called connects came rare, especially to younger guys my age. Having this access allowed me to rise to the level of "Big Timer" at the age of fifteen. I ended up being other guys' connect all throughout the city during that time. Just as with anything in this world, I had to form a crew to handle certain tasks. I started outshining everyone around with my lavish lifestyle. I had cars, motorbikes, and diamond jewelry just like the rappers I see today in videos.

I dated a lot of women, mainly women older than me from different walks of life. Life appeared to be so sweet at that time. I even owned two Rolex watches that I bought from someone on the black market. I had the best of everything in those times. I was like a celebrity of my times. I used to do things for the children of crack heads in the community as a form of my redemption for selling drugs. Eventually, I made two children that gave my life substance and made my mother a proud grandmother. As with anything else, my brother soon followed my pursuits and made his first child and my first niece. We were only sixteen and fifteen years of age. My mother was happy, but I think it was a gift and a curse to her because she was not yet even forty years old. Again, unbeknownst to any of us at the time there was a reason why we had to make children at such an early age when you look at how life happened to us years later.

It appeared to be the life every child or teen would want—Being the boss of their own lives, but at some point in my development into early manhood I began to feel sad. I guess the morals and principles that were instilled in me growing up started to resurface. I started to notice that all the community centers in the neighborhoods were closing. All the parks were being deserted, all my childhood friends were at war with each other over drugs and turf or territory that none of them owned. The two most devastating things to me to this day was how the mothers of friends I knew would sell their bodies for the drugs, and how many people I knew were dying everyday around me. More troubling is when I used to see some police officers arresting guys and some even made guys sell drugs for them. They would go to on to make busts at drug shops, only to get the drugs to put in their own drug shops. It was a very lucrative business, as I understand it now from a business perspective. I mean some shops used to sell up to $15,000 in drug sales a day. So, imagine the numbers on ten shops doing the same numbers or close. It would have been producing $150,000 per day and 4.5 million dollars a month in revenues— not profits. Crazy numbers, that convinces me that blacks are not poor. We just don't know what to do with all the money flowing through our communities.

I knew that I wanted a different life from what I was seeing around me. I didn't want to leave my children from being killed or going to prison for the rest of my life, so I made a decision to quit selling drugs. Honestly, it was a hard thing to do because I didn't know of any job or profession during those times of my limited knowledge that would match making thousands of dollars on the weekly or monthly basis. However, I still was motivated to quit. I told my girlfriend, Kendra Anderson, at that time I was quitting. She, even in her younger yet mature age encouraged me to do the right thing and quit. Then, I did and told my mother and everybody else. I still had plenty money put away to live off of while taking months to decide what I was going to do with my life. One day I called an old friend who I'll call Sidney Lewis. He was a guy that was heavy in the game at one time, but quit selling drugs and started his own business. We met in a restaurant that day. I'll never forget what he told me. "Rob, you are one the smartest youngsters I know and respect. You built an empire. All you have to do is do the same thing, but legally. You just have to figure it all out." He said in a mild but firm tone. He later took me to an old broken down house that he was investing in. He broke down the numbers on how much he was going to make on the deal and how much the house would be worth after he finished fixing it up. A process I understand now as flipping real estate and increasing the ARV (after market retail value) in real estate terms.

During that time I only understood it from a street hustler's perspective. In other words, I understood the math of it all—For I had mastered a trade of dealing with numbers in my head. This came from when I was in school. The math teacher would call me to the board in the front of the class to solve difficult math equations. I used to get stuck and embarrassed, so I would go home to study math problems in my head without using pencil or paper. In short, I did it to embarrass my teacher from always, as I seen it, trying to embarrass me. I would like to thank her for that, because it helped me to figure things out faster than most. I guess that's what allowed me to keep so many numbers in my head from my drug dealing days. Now, that I am a legit entrepreneur I can look at something and figure out the costs to make a profit all in my head. Again, it's amazing how certain experiences play significant roles in your life.

After I went back to living with my mother a light turned on in my head from a discussion Sidney and I had earlier. I wanted to flip houses and be a businessman. Realistically, I knew it would not just happen like that because I didn't have an education. This was one of the only times I felt bad about ever dropping out of school. For the most part, I knew I would have to go back to school and get my diploma and maybe go to college for real estate or business. In my immature mind, that was a long time away, and it was sort of an embarrassing notion of going back to high school at the age of eighteen in the eighth grade.

Months went by and I started to get assistance with getting into programs that would help me; things like vocational training or a program to get my GED. I even started doing work with my step dad to keep money coming. I still had some money, but it was going fast because nothing else was coming in. I even started to subsidize my lavish spending habits. I was spending time with my children and becoming a real father. Then suddenly out of nowhere the worst part of my life happened to me.

In the early morning hours of April 17, 1992, the New Orleans police came storming into my mother's house with weapons pointed at my family and me. I'd never seen so many officers in one place. We were confused and my mother asked respectfully and afraid, "What the hell is going on?"

One of the officers replied, " We are looking for your son, Robert Jones." I was confused and afraid, but assured them I was the person that they were looking for so they can stop pointing weapons at my family. They quickly arrested me, put me in handcuffs and told me I was under arrest. I asked them for what and they said armed robbery. I almost laughed, because I know I never robbed anyone and knew that they somehow made a mistake as my mother was telling them as well. I told my mother and family I would be right back once they realized that they had the wrong person for these crimes.

As we drove to the headquarters in silence, I still believed that I would be released soon. When I arrived at the station they seemed so jolly and happy that they had me in custody. They started questioning me saying that I killed some tourist, robbed some people and kidnapped and raped a woman. I thought it was a prank or something. For I never will or had to rape a woman because I had more women than maybe all the male officers there put together. Plus, I never killed or robbed anyone for I was a very successful drug dealer. At some point, I even told the latter to detectives after they insisted that I did commit those crimes.

They continued with the questioning until they finally realized that I had nothing to tell them. I was only telling them the truth—That I didn't commit any of these crimes that they accused me of. The crazy thing, one of the crimes from that April 1992 spree happened on April 6, 1992 —Three people were robbed and a woman was kidnapped and raped. This was totally insane to me, because I was at my son's first birthday party on that day with a lot of family and friends. The cops appeared to believe me at that time, so they focused on interrogating me about a tourist that had been shot and killed plus some additional robberies. I told them, "I did not do none of those crimes," but to no avail.

Then I saw all my friends, Donald Oliver, Pernell Harris and Christopher Borderer being rushed, in handcuffs, into the other rooms. I was sad to see them, but glad at the same time. Reason being, that maybe when they hear my friends tell them the same things I told them that they will then let us go home. Well, that thought went out the window when they hauled us down to central bookings. When I saw all the cameras and reporters as we walked to bookings, I knew that this was serious—And we'd been set up.

I remember first being able to call home. I told my mother and girlfriend that I had been charged with murder, kidnap, robbery and rape. They were disgusted and confused because they knew that I didn't do those kinds of things. They knew that was not my character and most of all who I was as a person. I was sent to Orleans Parish Prison (OPP) to wait until my fate was decided at my trial.

As the weeks turned into months, things got worse. My girlfriend came to visit me in the parish jail to tell me in such sad words, "I am pregnant," she said. I was glad and sad, because we had had plans on living a different life from how we were raised. We had plans to get married and buy our own home and live a successful life.

Months went by fast while I was still waiting to go to trial. We used all the money I had left plus money that my loved ones raised from friends and family to pay for some very expensive attorney fees, and put funds in my prison account to buy food out of the prison's commissary. This was mainly because I couldn't stomach the prison food. Then the holidays started to pass and everybody was missing me and I was missing them. Amazingly, on Christmas day of 1992, my youngest daughter was born. It was a joy, yet heartbreaking because I was not there. My girlfriend was left alone to care for my daughter and help out with my other two children that, technically, weren't hers. A hard task for any woman less along she was only sixteen years of age.

I went through four long years of frustration and moments of total despair because here I was in prison for crimes I didn't commit, and another guy, whom I didn't know was charged with the same crimes whom the prosecutors said was my partner in crime. It was horrible and mind blowing to be in that position. Unfortunately, life only got worse for me.

In March of 1996, I was a young 23 year old boy lost, confused and afraid standing before a judge and jury after a two-day trial. It was verdict time and I was awaiting my fate. I felt in a small way that I would not get found guilty because I was innocent, but I knew of some guys that had been convicted even though they said they were innocent too.

The courtroom was filled to the max with my friends and family. The jury came in and the judge made everyone stand for the verdict. Facing me, he read, "As to all counts that you have been charged with Mr. Jones, the jury finds you guilty of all counts."

My face dropped and my family shouted sounds of disbelief and burst into tears. I was numb. I asked my attorney what he'd said. My attorney responded, "Guilty." I turned to look at my family, but held back my tears. I smiled and said that everything will be okay. I said that to reassure them, but inside I was devastated and broken. That day I experienced death on another level, while still alive. I was sentenced a couple of days later for robbery, kidnap, and rape.

Then the murder case came up for sentencing. The prosecutor was talking to my lawyer who had came to me, and they both, in their own ways, convinced me to take a deal on the murder charge, not knowing until years later that someone else had been convicted and sentenced for the same murder. Also unbeknownst to me, that same person had admitted to the prosecutor the morning of my trial that I'd had nothing to do with the crimes. Since I had just been convicted of a rape I hadn't committed, I was afraid, so I signed the deal on the murder case, but I never admitted to anything. The judge sentenced me to life without parole for the rape and 25 years for one count of kidnapping, and three counts of robbery and 21 years for the murder—A total of life plus 121 years to serve in prison. I looked around and saw my mother and girlfriend sitting in the courtroom. I thought that would be the last time I'd ever see them again.

Somewhat accepting my new reality of being sentenced to die in prison for crimes I didn't commit, I began preparing my mind for the next journey of my life. I was headed for Angola State Penitentiary, or the

"Big House," as they called it. I had heard many stories of the place. At that time, it was considered the bloodiest prison in America—Where guys would get killed or just die in prison. I knew only two things for certain, one, that I was somehow going to get out of prison one day, I just didn't know how, and two, that I was going to go there as a man and leave as a man no matter what I had to do to defend myself.

Fortune or streaks of luck always seemed to fall in my lap when I needed them most. Instead of being sent immediately to Angola like most who received a life sentence. I remained in Orleans Parish Prison (OPP) for months. There, a guy whom I'll call Tony Steward came into to be housed in the cell I shared with two other men. It was a privilege cell because I was the tier representative. Tony was an old convict serving 20 years of a life sentence from Angola trying to give his life sentence back. He knew my family and uncles that had also been in Angola for years, of whom I'd actually forgotten about until he mentioned it. Sad, but it's the truth. Over the next few weeks he taught me everything I needed to know—Even down to how to use a prison knife to defend myself in case it came down to that. I was like a cadet in the military training for war. Unfortunately, his appeal was denied and he was shipped back to Angola. He and I are friends to this day. I am out of prison, but he is still there serving a life sentence with no way out of prison. Breaks my heart to even write this, because he already served over 40 years incarcerated this date—Too long for a person to be dead let alone in prison, in my opinion.

Maybe months later, I was to shipped to Angola. When I arrived there I really felt like a slave watching prisoners dressed like slaves with the straw hats, working in the cotton fields. I couldn't believe my eyes seeing all that land and looking at the guards riding on horses carrying shotguns like in old slave movies. The only thing was missing were the whips that were used to beat disobedient slaves. I knew that it was going to be a long ride for me there. However, I was ready and equipped for that ride to the best of my knowledge. I was ready to make my showing, to let everyone know that I was not one to be played with, just as I'd made my stand in the OPP when I got there. I eventually got that chance just weeks into my stay. I put my boxing skills to good use. It was only years later that I was actually forced to use a weapon to defend myself, but no one, including myself was seriously hurt. Overall, I achieved my respect and never had any other problems on those levels.

I met up with my lost uncles and we lived around each other for months. I started to notice that a lot the prisoners around me that had been in for more than 20 years were lost, crazy and completely hopeless. No family alive, no visits, no money, no support; just completely lost. It was a feeling I couldn't understand at the time until it started happening to me. I slowly started losing contact with friends and family whom seemed to have forgotten about me. Then, if it couldn't get any worse, I called home and found out that my younger brother, Pierre, had been killed. I dropped the phone and walked back to my cell. I was totally devastated and crushed. I cried all that night and did not even go to work in the fields the next morning. I walked the prison yard grounds alone, thinking and hurting. This went on for a few days, especially since I was not even allowed to go to his funeral. Family and friends came to visit and console me as well as my incarcerated friends, but none of it mattered, mainly because I felt responsible for his death. I also felt responsible for the death of my brother-in-law who was killed that same year because both he and my brother were selling drugs trying to raise money to get me out of prison. Their actions are no way being justified here, but that was all they knew how to do to make fast money, and get the amount of money I needed to hire a good attorney. It really was a sad time for me.

One day while walking the prison yard something happened that changed my life forever. A boxer trainer friend I'd met while there walked up to me and said, "Hey Rob, I see you are going through it...but know that life is like boxing. Life is going to throw you some hard blows, but you must throw counter punches back. Either you fight back or let life knock you out."

I truly understood what he was trying to say from a boxer's perspective. In simple terms, he was telling me to fight back. I took that advice and decided that I was going to fight my way out of prison. I knew I'd have to do it myself because I was not going to have the funds for an attorney since my family was poor and my younger brother and brother-in-law, now deceased, had been my only financial resource.

I knew that I had to master the law, but first I had to get my GED. I immediately got transferred to the main prison where all the education was and enrolled in a literacy program. They started me at a third grade level. I was reluctant at first, but I went with it and passed those classes quickly. It was easy of course because I was not a complete dummy. However, it got harder when I made it to GED school.

In 1999, I got my GED and was so proud and happy. I sent a copy of the diploma to my mother and all my family members. They were proud of me. However, I didn't stop there. I had also been studying the law at the same time while in the GED school. I went on to spend my own money sent from family and friends on books and took college level correspondence courses. Some of the courses I even got for free because I wrote to colleges and practically begged them for the courses I couldn't afford. I studied criminal law, civil law, tort law, family law, real estate law, business law, journalism, business administration, political science, public communication and many other subjects all, on my own free time. I used to read a self-help book a day for seven years straight. I was doing it all while still working as a prisoner. I joined self-help organizations and surrounded myself with what prisoners call political prisoners, who in my understanding were the smart guys who offered assistance to other prisoners. As a matter of fact, every single one of the guys whom I surrounded myself are now free. They found a way out of prison, and so did I. I would say I chose the right crowd to follow this time around in life.

Over the next few years I remained on a mission to get out of prison. I was filing my own pleadings in court as well as helping other prisoners file their pleadings. At that time, I was not yet even documented as 'inmate counsel,' whose job it was to file inmate pleadings in courts. However, I was smart and started winning guys cases. It was amazing because I won pleadings at that time in two circuit courts and one in the Louisiana Supreme court for other prisoners.

One inmate received a new trial and the other two ended up with lesser sentences that made their stay in prisoner shorter. Despite those successes, I couldn't seem to get wins in my own cases. I realized that I needed outside help to get out, so I started writing attorneys, investigators, judges, preachers, organizations and even the District Attorney's office pleading my innocence. I couldn't understand it, here I was a moderate prisoner with no rule infractions or violations in years. I had more education under my belt than some college students, but I couldn't get help to get out of prison. It was confusing because I was doing everything right.

My family helped as much as they could with some cheap attorney fees in a few of my court appearances from pleadings I'd filed in court. I did all the work and would hire an attorney to argue before the court. Even then, I still had to step in at times to co-counsel alongside of them. Basically, I was paying them for doing nothing.

Eventually, I met an investigator who was hired by this girl I was dating. He did a great job finding some undisclosed evidence in my case, but he eventually became frustrated and discouraged because the Orleans District Attorney's office was playing hardball and refusing to completely cooperate with him. As a result, it set me back years of litigating and finally losing again in the courts. Thereafter, I was introduced to these grassroots (I was not given permission to disclose these groups and people's real names) organizations that helped inmates in need. I offered to assist them in some legal research for their clients and our relationship was born from there.

Things were shaping up because the Innocence Project of New Orleans (IPNO) also came upon my case and searched for the DNA evidence that I asked in a pro se pleading to be preserved. Well, that didn't work out because they were informed that the DNA evidence and the case files had all been lost. Personally, I thought that it had been destroyed because those two articles of evidence would undoubtedly prove my innocence. Years later, I would find out that I wasn't too far off the mark.

Over the next few years, the grassroots organization's director, Gloria Jackson (which is not her real name) and I became real close and developed a bond as we both fought many battles trying to obtain my freedom. I soon learned the power of the word "denied" as I continued to fight for my freedom as an innocent man. As I explained to Gloria I needed someone with enough resources to win. The organization went over and beyond with limited resources, but I needed an army of attorneys to fight the big bad criminal justice monster. Eventually, after I got denied on one of what i thought was my last round in the courts the Innocence Project New Orleans came back on my case, this time to fight it as a Brady violation—meaning when the state withholds favorable evidence from a defendant.

I'll never forget, it was the year 2010 when Innocence Project New Orleans found some new documents that proved my innocence. I was excited and ready to go back into court with this arsenal of evidence to finally get my freedom. When the time came, I would learn that I would be denied once again. It was so heartbreaking because we had all the evidence, but the courts still denied my petition. Although it was frustrating, I knew at some point from a legal perspective I would eventually win the case because I had the right facts to match the law that applied.

Well, that fight took many more years before I began to see any light. In the meantime, I somewhat started preparing for what I wanted to do once I got out of prison. I knew that I wanted to start and operate my own business, but that didn't seem like enough. I was busy trying to figure it all out while anticipating a victory in the courts, when something happened that gave me some clarity.

I was awoken by a friend, Tyron Arthur. He got me out of bed to go to the TV room in the prison dormitory where we both were being housed with more than fifty other prisoners. As I entered the room I saw on the news that some young boys had been shot multiple times in the head in our hometown of New Orleans. This was a regular thing to both of us, but what made this one different is that these kids were burned after being shot or while being shot; I don't quite remember the order. This was so sad to me and I felt sorry for their families. At that junction in my life, I decided that I wanted to do something to stop these young black boys from killing each other like that. I had already studied history and knew how racism played a major role in the history of black people in this country, but I needed to find out who was behind the schemes to keep black boys killing each other like animals and going to jail like it was legal.

Most importantly, I wanted to find a solution to the problem. It gave me another mission while still fighting to get out of prison. I studied every book and material on the subject, but still did not find any real solutions. I communicated and talked to some very intellectual people on the matter, but still found no real explanations or solutions.

During a visit with an investigator friend, I met Jerome Morgan who I knew from prison years before the meeting. We were mutual friends of quite a few people. He and I also used to meet when we visited our attorneys from IPNO. He was fighting his case as an innocent man too. We had the very same issues, in my opinion, as mostly poor black males in this country—Brady Violations of the 14th amendment to the United States constitution. We discussed problems with the youth and what could we do once we got out of prison. At that time, we both had our cases pending, awaiting rulings.

In my continuous efforts to find a solution to solve black-on-black crimes concerning the youth, my studies led me to some very interesting revelations that showed that black men and especially black boys were the targets of a diabolical system of racist groups of people. The alarming thing was that it didn't matter what color you were to be a part of this machine, as I'll call it. I learned that racism was not an individual thing, but a group matter, systematically created. It was the work of some sick people, mainly whites, trying to preserve a certain way of life to keep themselves above blacks and make all young black males their slaves. They didn't worry too much about the black woman, which explains why black women have better jobs than the black males in this country, even to this date. In other words, these systems are created to strip the black males of their manhood and reverse the role of the males and females. I get so disgusted when I hear how men stay home now and watch the children while the women go to work to provide for the households. That is sick and not cool at all.

This process all began with an old white slave owner named Willie Lynch. He went to the Colony of Virginia to show other slave owners his methods on how he broke his slaves in the West Indies. He noticed while there that too many of the male slaves were hanging from trees. He told the slave owners that they were losing profits. Then, he proceeded to show them his methods.

He explained that if you take the strongest male slaves and literally rip them apart with two horses tied on different ends while his children, other slaves and mainly his woman watch, that it would strike fear in them, that the mother will break her own sons in fear that they would end up like their father. He also showed how to divide them by using the color of their skin, showing the lighter ones more favor than the darker ones, treating the ones whose hair were better than the rest by having the slave owners sleep with the woman slaves, then breed the lighter skin ones together until they look white.

He told them to cause distrust amongst the female and males by impregnating the female and forcing her to keep quiet until the baby was born. While the male slave waited nine months to see his child, only to find out that his woman was sleeping with a white slave master—That would break them apart for good. He said that doing this would last for at least a thousand years.

I read the Willie Lynch letter and don't know how accurate it is as far as authenticity, however, I know that it has some truths to it, because I can see the consequences of his work in the actions of black people today. You see it in our trust issues, hatred for each other and lack of love for our own lives.

The next thing I read about was the supposed Emancipation Proclamation in 1865 when the slaves were freed. Immediately, the system went to work using the 13th Amendment as their rule of law. This basically states that no one should be forced into involuntary servitude unless they are convicted of a crime. This set in motion the black code laws that were used to justify locking black males up by the thousands all over the country.

Then I learned about the Jim Crow laws, and now the new Jim Crow laws that we see today. For it is no coincidence that black males make up the majority of prisoners in a country where blacks are considered a minority. This here, my friends, is by design. These schemes are real and will take more than the few pages I have left to finish this part. However, I will give you enough information to see the light.

The people behind these seemingly crafty schemes had become scientists, so I had to become a scientist to understand this stuff. The schemes are set in place to directly affect the four basic needs of every human being. It is a proven fact that most agree that there are four basic needs for every human, no matter what color you are.

The first basic need is the need to survive. Every human as well as animals have a basic need for survival. That need includes, having food, clothing and other things to live life. One will just about do anything to satisfy the need for survival.

Now, how does this relate to young black boys? I'll explain. Whether one believes it or not, but everything we have in America will boil down to dollar and cents. The food a person needs costs, clothing costs, a home costs and other essentials cost. So, when a father is removed from the household from drug addiction, jail or death, it leaves the single parent mother there to fulfill her child's needs for survival. In most cases I know, when a mother can't fulfill her child's needs for survival, he generally seeks to fulfill that need outside of the house. I am not talking about babies or small children. I am speaking of young black teens or tweens who are basically caught up in the latest fashion trends and desire to live life above their means or means of their parent.

The next step for the young black boy is to seek to satisfy this basic need by asking other relatives for money or these things that he sees as a necessity. When that fails as my experiences tell me, the black boy starts looking in his environment for answers. As result, when he sees boys his age or older getting money and getting the materialistic things that he desires too, he begins to mimic what he sees. He tries stealing, robbing, killing or selling drugs until he finds one route that works. Many people can argue that they have a choice, which is true. However, they don't produce the tons of drugs flooding the black communities. They don't make the military style weapons that are used to take other black lives and they don't control the media who perpetuate a lavish lifestyle to these young boys. In no way, do I justify their actions, but I understand the need that things effect and how survival tactics—any means necessary, comes into play. It's like telling a hungry lion not to eat a deer that's passing right in front of him.

The second need is the need to be loved. Every person in this world desires to be loved. Love is such a powerful need—you cannot live without love. Even animals need to receive affection and love. Often, human beings misunderstand love. Honestly, I can understand why. Just think when someone tells you, "I love you." The word love in this context is being used as a verb; which is an action word. So, people think love is when you can do something for them. In other words, showing them by doing for them. As it relates to the young black boy when his poor mother can't get the things that he wants, let alone the things he needs, it can be easily misconstrued that his parent doesn't love him like the next boy's parent who gets her son everything that he wants. I know this from experience.

Also, when parents fuss at or call the boy degrading names comparing him to his dad who is deemed by a scratched mother, as no good. I hear these tones right to this day. "You ain't shit," "You make me sick," or "I hate you." These words tell the mind that there is no love there. Thus, the boy seeks love from the outside. Most of the time it's with other boys experiencing the same things at home and they can be there for each other to show comfort. As it relates to little girls—They end up sleeping with different boys or older men trying to satisfy the need to be loved.

The third need is the need to learn. Every human desires to learn more. Learning allows a person to move forward in life. This is evident in the growth and development of a child. A child comes into this world not knowing anything until he mimics what he learns from others. So, when the single mother is forced to work two jobs or is just not there to teach her son, he will learn it from someone else. This is just not about academics as most would think. The young black boy needs learn how to survive in the real world, something that schools does not give him. For the most part, if he is poor more than likely he is going to an inadequate school per national standards. Again, he will seek the advice or game from the hustlers in the neighborhood. Please don't misconstrue what I am trying to say here. I am not saying that some black boys don't go in the right direction. I am speaking of the majority here; because the evidence is in their actions and the statistics you read every day. It's bad when other black boys kill more black boys in neighborhoods than soldiers in war are killed in the same year.

The fourth basic need is the need to belong to a bigger cause. This is powerful to me because everybody wants to be a part of something. Most people choose religion, organizations, or businesses. When the young black boy is not a part of something with a bigger cause he generally forms his own crew or joins a gang. I guess it explains also why most white children, especially boys, are enrolled in some sort of organization. I can attest to how much the role of belonging to a community group impacted my life and others. I know guys that never seen the inside of prison to this day. Well, I can see why today a lot of our black youth are not a part of programs. Simple, there are not many in the poor black communities anymore. As a matter of fact, I do not even see many vocational schools near these areas as much as they used to be. So, it explains why there are so many gangs amongst our youth today in the city of New Orleans and across the country.

All these basic needs play a major role in how these kids act. I will refute this with anybody because I did my research. I don't care about being right, but I do care about telling the truth.

The next phase is the finishing touches. If you noticed that when all the four basic needs above were not satisfied the boy went to the environment. The environment has its own set of rules. Let me break it down for you. Laws are external forces outside the human being. Values are internal forces inside the human being. Basically, everything in this world is based upon laws, principles and values. How does this come into play? Well, once the environment controls the four basics needs of the young black boy, it begins to perpetuate its external laws, internally. Thus, the boy adopts the laws as his values and acts out what he now believes are his core values. In other words, the environment says that he is a gangster who has no regard for human life. If he adopted the law as his value he would have no regards for human life.

This is wrong and it must stop. Racist people are using their powers, positions and wealth to keep this going. If black people don't take a stand to start fixing their own problems, one day we all are going to wake up and all our young black males are going to be dead.

I read an article in the Advocate newspaper of Louisiana that made me feel good about my research on this matter. It read in parts that Louisiana ranks amongst the worst states in the nation when it comes to the wellbeing of its children per the Annie E. Casey Foundation kid count data book released July 22, 2014. Most of the state's poor showing relates to children living in poverty and in single parent homes. 36 percent of Louisiana's children live in families where no parent has year round full time employment. That rate is five percent higher than the nation average. The article further reads, that the above statistics on child wellbeing is based upon four different areas: Economic wellbeing (like the need to survive), education (like the need to learn), health and family (like the need to love and be loved) and community (like the need to want to be a part of a bigger cause).

In conclusion, in 2013, Jerome Morgan and I went to court together. He won a new trial in his case and immediately got out of prison on bail. After several years the state finally dismissed the case against him in May 2016. As for me, my case was denied and I was sent back to Angola.

Finally, on November 20, 2015, I was released on bail, awaiting a new trial. Then, on my birthday, January 26, 2017, the state dropped the charges on me. When I walked out of prison there were so many cameras and people there waiting on me, including Jerome Morgan and Daniel Rideau. I knew Daniel from prison when he had been serving a life sentence that he gave back in 2003.

The three of us met and hung out regularly and started talking about forming an organization. Well, that is how Free-Dem Foundations, Inc. was born. Today, we work with youth by mentoring them and teaching them skills to survive in the real world. We also teach them how to be responsible men and to work towards the ownership of themselves and businesses. We fulfill their four basic needs to be loved, to learn, to survive and to belong to a bigger cause.

Doing this changes their environment into a more productive place. Thus, they adopt the rules in the environment that we create for them. It allows them to adopt those rules and act totally different from most. We know that it works because we have living proof in the young men we've developed. Too many more young black boys are still falling through the cracks, but our resolve to help them is unbreakable.

—Robert Jones

Daniel's Story

As I reflect upon my childhood I can precisely point out factors that directly influenced my behavior throughout my life. I intend to use my life as a study to deter youths from experiencing the many tribulations I have endured, also hoping that my story will enlighten adults of the various traps that have been set by numerous institutions. I believe that no child or adult chooses a life of crime, but on the contrary, in every instance, there are incidents or circumstances, which lead a person to choose crime as a way of life.

I am the second of five siblings, first boy and the second oldest. In 1975 my mother moved from Palmetto, Louisiana, in search of a better life, her two kids in tow, my oldest sister Kawana and I. My father is and has been non-existent in my life; never even got a single word of advice from the man. Although I have met him a time or two, he abandoned my mom with two infants. He claimed my sister as his own and I was his, maybe.

The last time I heard from him, incidentally, was when I was in Angola serving a life sentence without parole and running out of appeals. I had reached the Louisiana Supreme Court on my post conviction relief, meaning my next step was the Federal Court and only if I could meet the time limitations which were breathing down my neck.

It was then that I pleaded with my mom to get me an attorney. Unbeknownst to be, at this particular time, my father was in New Orleans at my mom's house. When she brought up the topic to him, he responded by saying, "If it is meant for Daniel to come home he will. Don't waste your money." That was the last time that my mother saw him.

The First Twelve Years

I was about a year old when my mother married Russell, hereby referred to as 'step dad.' He was the son of a Baptist pastor. Step dad was a very angry person that physically abused me the first twelve years of my life. What caused my step dad to treat a child so cruelly is beyond me.

On one particular day my mother was at work and my step dad was left to babysit me. We were at my step dad's parents' big beautiful house. No one knows what really happened, some say that my step dad hit me, he said I fell out of my crib, but in any event, I ended up in intensive care unit with blunt trauma to my liver. I was only 18 months old and almost died from my injuries. As I laid there in that bed fighting for my life, my mom said that I crossed my leg, kicked back and smiled at her. In hindsight I realize that even then God was instilling in me the strength needed to make it through the next 11 years.

According to most experts, a child's brain develops at its quickest pace between the ages of zero through five, and that 80 percent of an 18 year old's intelligence is obtained in the first six years. Experiencing childhood trauma and adversity, such as physical or sexual abuse, is a risk factor for borderline personality disorder, depression, anxiety, and other psychiatric disorders. One study using ACE data found that roughly 54 percent of cases of depression and 58 percent of suicide attempts in women were connected to adverse childhood experiences (Felitti & Anda, 2009). Child maltreatment also negatively impacts the development of emotion regulation, which often persists into adolescence or adulthood (Messman-Morre, Walsh, & DiLillo, 2010).

The first twelve years of my life were horrible, filled with physical abuse and neglect. I reflect upon these memories of childhood in an effort to give one insight into the influences that directly affected me as an adult. This will be a difficult task considering the fact that it will be the first time that I have attempted to put these memories together, but mostly because my family and friends know nothing of this, especially my mother, whose love gave me the courage to make it through those difficult times. My mother was and still is ignorant to most of the abuse that was dealt to me, as she was going through abuse at the same time.

My step dad was a very mean man and for the life of me I cannot see what my mom saw in this man. My mother went on to have three more children with this man, my two younger sisters and my brother. I love my siblings all the same, but their dad was my enemy number one. Despite my step dad's father being a pastor of a Baptist church, my step dad was a self proclaimed Rastafarian who didn't come to church with us. He quit the family's landscaping business and basically became a substance abuser, which lead to his demise. I can remember countless times where he beat my mom with his fists like she was a man. My mom, my older sister Kawana, and myself were all terrified of this man. My mom tried her best for us not to see all that was going on, but what she didn't know was that there were also things going on that she had no knowledge of.

Although many of these memories come in blurs, and I am unable to remember most accounts, I will try to compile these reflections to the best of my ability. One thing I am certain of is that I don't ever remember any happy times inside of my home. There was never a time in my childhood where I felt safe and secure.

Let me begin by saying that I was a very troubled kid growing up. I was suspended 27 times in elementary school starting in kindergarten. I can remember kicking my kindergarten teacher for being mean to me and allowing everyone to skip me in the line to get on the swing. No matter what happened at school, I can't remember a time when anybody tried to find out why I behaved the way I did. When I got home my mom would fuss sometimes and when I did something outrageous she would whip me. What she didn't know was that when she went to bed and slept, my nightmares began.

The Laundry Room

My siblings and I shared a big room in the back of the house on Soniat Street. I can remember my mom going to school and sometimes working two and three jobs, but at night when everyone was asleep my step dad would wake me and bring me in the laundry room and abuse me in ways that no child should endure. At first I can remember being made to bend over and take hit after hit from belts, switches, extension cords and such. Many times I got in trouble in school for not staying in my seat, not because I wanted to cause havoc, but because I could not take the pain of sitting. My step dad hit me so vigorously, with so much evil intent that the thought of it today still sometimes bring chills to my soul. As I remember the look in his eyes, it was as if I was looking at the devil himself. As I got older the abuse got worse. I remember him striking blows to my body as if I was a grown man, one time my arm being put in a sling. My oldest sister would cry me to sleep at night; she would be waiting on me when I came from the laundry. There were countless nights where I lay awake waiting for him to come get me. Many times my mom would physically discipline me for something I had done at school, but he still would come get me and beat me again.

Below is a passage from my oldest sister Kawana Rideau Evans that details her recollection of events:

"I remember looking forward to watching cartoons on Saturday mornings with my brother. As we waited for our parents to awake we would spend that time making each other laugh. The contagious laughter became problematic because Daniel's laugh was more of a pig's snort and the anxiety of awakening our parents became a game that we played. One morning in particular, the laughter caused my stepfather to awaken and he came into my grandparent's guest room where we slept, furious with us because we were not asleep. I vividly remember him picking up the five-inch thick Bible that sat on the chest of drawers and suddenly the laughter immediately silenced. As I watched in horror, he forcefully hit my brother on the head and then turned to me. My brother's lick wasn't shocking, but the fact that he hit me was. This was the one and only time I can remember that my stepfather hit me. I wish I could say the same for my brother.

"My brother and I always shared a room and in this particular shot gun house our room was all the way to the back next to the kitchen. We slept comfortably on a pull out sofa bed where almost every night we would lay in bed fearing what was to come. The sound of my step father's thong beach slippers terrified us both, but not nearly as much as what that sound meant in the middle of the night. Even as an adult the thought of that sound still causes me to cringe to this day. I would try my hardest to cheer my brother up, however he ended up comforting me more than anything. With a mere pat on my brother's shoulder he knew to get up and walk quietly to the washroom. Never flinching, crying or showing any sense of fear, he was a true soldier. I could hear the muffled sounds of the hit and my brother's yelling, and just like that it was over. My brother would get back in the bed warning me to be quiet, so that I would not be hurt. I have replayed those horrible nights over and over many times and I know that my brother took those beatings in stride to protect me."

Touch the Line

I have always been an adventurous boy; I loved to be outside playing with my best friend Micey who lived up the street. Our neighborhood was a tight knit group and we could basically roam around an eight-block radius. It was a nice summer day and we had a big football game going down on Robert Street that was in full effect after dusk. I remember my step dad telling me to make sure I came home before it got dark because I was supposed to be punished and he didn't want my mom to know he let me go outside to play. The game was good and I lost track of time, so my step dad came to look for me. By the time he found me he was so angry that when I saw him I knew there was a price to pay. I had to be about eleven at the time and physical abuse had become a way of life for me. Although I cannot remember all that he said the gist was that he had to hear my mom's mouth because he let me go play, and now I had to pay for being hard headed.

I remember starting at the corner of Robert Street and Soniat Street—being hit with a switch, with my pants down, at every line in the sidewalk on the entire block. It was days before I could sit down because the pain was unbearable. I cannot remember certainly, but I can vaguely remember my mom tending to my wounds. I didn't go to school for a few days and I stayed home with my step dad's cousin Dot. This was around the time of the separation, which caused us to run to the battered women's shelter on Carrollton Avenue, where we stayed for a couple of weeks.

During those last years, as those beatings became more frequent for my mother, I can remember thinking of the day that I would kill my step dad. There were many times as I was going through puberty, that I tried to fight with him to get off my mom, both my sister Kawana and I. My step dad kept a shotgun in the closet, and I would sometimes play with it when no one was around. My step dad also had a pellet gun that he used to let me shoot, but I knew I had to shoot him with the double barrel shotgun with two triggers. I would point it at the mirror and click it; that's how I was going to kill him.

As I reflect on that last beating that my mom took, he was choking my mom with a phone cord and my sister and I tried to help my mom, to no avail. My mom's eyes were rolling to the back of her head, so I went to the closet and got that gun. I looked everywhere for shells but couldn't find any. My step dad took the gun from me and said he would kill us all. He must have knocked me out because I have only vague memories of how we ended up at the shelter that night, but the next morning would end the first twelve years.

I only gave you a few instances of some abuse given to me and my mother because if I try to reflect too much it brings back feelings I don't necessarily care to feel, yet I hope someone can benefit from my experiences. My quest is to end the destruction of our youth by the systems of oppression. To help the young black man understand within him is the power to do all he wants and needs. In terms of education people tend to say it starts at home, and I agree. I also would like to point out; the first twelve years of a child's life are critical in terms of thought process. Many wonder how the youth can do some of the things they do, yet I challenge one to disagree, remembering in most cases something significant had happened at home, sometimes more severe than others. In my case, I would like to hope my case was one of the more severe cases, yet I understand there are countless worse cases. I was never raped or molested, thank God, but I was deprived of my childhood.

We were on welfare and I was the only boy in the middle of three girls, I grew up wearing hand me downs and something new on holidays. Although there was a man physically present, I did not have a real man's presence in my life. In hindsight, I realize all the main characteristics I have came from my step dad's father, the Baptist pastor hereafter referred to as my grandfather. I realize I had a bond with this man that was greater than anything. Not only did I get male nurturing from him, he also introduced me to God and laid a solid foundation for my faith. My grandfather was an upstanding man in the community and a businessman. He had a landscaping business that was prosperous when he was in health to work and manage the business.

I used to work every summer there after I was ten years old. I used to make forty dollars a day, which was good money at the time. I looked forward to those summers. It kept some money in my pockets. My grandfather was also a critical thinker. I remember taking long walks with him as he observed nature, his mind constantly wandering in thought. My step dad was the exact opposite of his father, where he was mean spirited; my grandfather was gentle and nurturing.

We lived in the next block from my grandfather's house. So many days I went there for refuge. Of course, my step dad was never there with us, I was happy about that and I never wanted to leave my grandparent's house.

I remember the day my auntie came got us from the battered woman's shelter on Carrollton Avenue; it was one of the happiest days of my young life. We were going to live with one of my favorite cousins, and away from this place that seemed dreary and like a jail.

I can't remember exactly how long we lived there but it was at least a year. Everything was good at first, but then it seemed as though we were more of a burden. I could tell the way my cousins started to act with their belongings, for they had everything and we had nothing. We had left everything except the bags of clothes that we took along with us.

In my mind my cousins had everything. They were involved in all types of activities from ballet to karate; had all the latest shoes, clothes and accessories. It almost felt as though we were second-class because my mom had five kids and needed welfare to support us. In hindsight I know we were waiting for housing assistance from the government. When it came through, we moved to Valence Street, not too far from my grandfather's church.

After that I went from school to school, getting expelled for fighting along the way. Despite having to fight almost every week, I did manage to graduate in 1988.

Jumping Off the Porch

Jumping off the porch is a decision, and that decision is to pick wrong over right. I had been dabbling with this decision since I was twelve, stealing bikes here and there and doing mischievous things, which could have been corrected. My step dad did nothing to nurture me, a growing boy reaching puberty. So, at the age of 13 I was coming home from school, and I didn't have my "boss," (my oldest sister Kawana) with me, so I definitely was on the loose! I got off the Regional Transit Authority (RTA) bus on Washington and Lasalle and decided to walk to the store on Feret and Washington to buy something. To my surprise, I walked up on a boy from the Magnolia projects hitting the Lay's potato chip truck right there by the store. As I was approaching them I was presented with the decision, shall I jump off the porch or shall I stay on? If only I would have had some type of positive influence to offset the abuse I had endured since a toddler, or the comfort of experiencing complete love at home. I jumped off that porch.

As I snatched two boxes of chips in broad day light, I made a quick decision not to follow the group of boys running across the street to the project (who all got away) and instead followed a boy down Feret street and into Woodson Middle School. Obviously, he was from the neighborhood cause he hit a few hallways and left me lost in the school. I had to stash the chips, and as I was trying to find an exit I got jammed up by the police that were looking for us. The police questioned me and I denied knowing anything. I had watched old movies like Scarface and heard the old school guys give the game, I knew the rule: "when the cops got you, you don't know nothing and never snitch under no circumstances." So although I did not have a logical explanation for being in the school, I stuck to my story that I didn't know anything about a potato chip truck. That meant I didn't go to juvenile detention this time, but the police made my mom come get me from the school. I told my mom basically the same story I told the police and my mom whipped me with a belt. This was shortly after my mom left my step dad, so by this time my mom's whippings were pointless. I realized that my mom could not do anything to me in terms of hurting me because my step dad had been issuing beatings five times worse.

With this newfound freedom I decided to really indulge into criminal behavior whenever I got the chance. My next run-in with the police was at a department store. My birthday is November 27th, and the great thing about my birthday is that it sometimes fell on thanksgiving or the same weekend and it's always on or around the Bayou Classic. Furthermore, this is my favorite part of the year and my mom gave me a hundred dollars to get me an outfit. I was fourteen and my mom was attempting to give me some freedom, so she let me go to Canal Street on my own. By this time I had been various times without my mom knowing, which included an all expenses paid trip to the World's Fair, where a friend and I jumped on the street car without paying and came home with pockets full of change from the wishing well at the age of 10.

So I went into Foot Locker expecting to get me some kicks and still have some money to get a shirt. K-Swiss was a hot shoe at the time and I had to have the all black high top. I had to. Ever since my mom left Russell she had been working two and three jobs to make ends meet. I bought the all black K-Swiss and it felt so good to finally go and buy exactly what I wanted—too good! I had almost thirty dollars left to get the rest of my outfit for my birthday. Next stop, D. H. Holmes. I could find a cheap shirt in there. So my friend and I went straight to the polo's. Like most boys 14 years old I allowed the value of material things supersede what was right, and I decided to steal a Ralph Lauren striped polo. As I quickly folded the shirt and put it in the bag with my shoes, I looked around to see if someone had seen. Feeling that I was undetected, I made my way to the escalator thinking this is too easy. As we approached the end of the escalator two men appeared from nowhere and were looking right at me. At that very moment, I knew that I had been caught red handed. They took us to the security room and I got the shock of a lifetime. As I walked in with my hands cuffed behind my back, I saw about fifty monitors connected to cameras spread about the store. There I learned two things: someone is always watching, and I would not steal out of a department store again. The department store gave me a warning and called my mom to come and get me.

My story was that my friend was doing the stealing, and I stuck to it. I don't think I even got a whipping for this incident. I was 14 and I think my mom realized the whippings weren't doing any good. Sometime soon thereafter my mom moved to Carrollton, it was there I found acceptance and I finally felt validity.

The Graveyard

The Graveyard is a small neighborhood in Carrollton that is about the size of a 10-block radius. It runs from Broadway Street to Carrollton Avenue and from South Claiborne to Oak Street. The Graveyard was a tight knit neighborhood in Carrollton. It was called the Graveyard because there is a cemetery in the neighborhood that is divided by its major street, Hickory. My mom and Josh, her man at the time, found a house on Fern Street and we quickly settled in. The neighbors were friendly and there were plenty of kids on the block to play with. Two doors down lived my friend Damon who quickly became my brother-in-law after he impregnated my sister with her first child. Big Damon was well respected in the neighborhood and he was about four years older than me. He quickly took me under his wing and introduced me to the neighborhood. Once I got acquainted with the Graveyard Posse (GYP) boys I became one of them and we were like family. The older guys looked out for the younger and were quick to give advice, no matter what you did. You had to respect the elders or somebody would get you straight.

I went on my first hustle with an O.G. named Cleve. Cleve was older than me and he was nothing less than a bully. He rode around with two pair of boxing gloves in his car and would challenge anybody anywhere, from uptown to downtown, to fight. Cleve stood about 6"2' and weighed about 225, and had an aggressive attitude to match. Cleve was a burglar by occupation, but most thought he was a big time drug dealer. He kept a nice ride and kept a new pair of Bally's on his feet, and I would always ask him to bring me on a hustle. That day finally came when I was about 15.

I skipped school to joyride in a stolen car that my friends and me had taken the night before. I spotted Cleve walking on Adams towards Niggatown[1] and pulled up to him. He said he had a hustle set up and needed a ride. I said, "I'm down." It was a house in Niggatown and we went through the alley and up the back steps. After about 20 seconds he kicked the back door once and it flew open. We rushed in and he told me to go to the front and watch through the window. He began to disassemble the electronics in the living room, and then told me to check the bedrooms. I went into a bedroom and found a chrome .38 and some jewelry. He got other things as well. We put everything into pillowcases and sheets, loaded the car and were off. Cleve had a friend that bought all his electronics, so he let me have the gun and the jewelry, which made me a proud gun owner at the age of 15. This was the first of many burglaries, coupled with my newfound skill of stealing cars. I was starting to get the hang of this thing called crime.

Tarpon Land

My freshmen year at Alcee Fortier High School went pretty smooth other than an ongoing feud between the 13th ward and the 17th ward. Unfortunately, I spent my first 12 years being raised in the 13th and I knew everybody, but I have been living in the 17th for the last couple of years and my allegiance was with them because I learned the game there. So, I had to chose sides; was I from the 13th where I was born and raised? Or was I from the Graveyard where they adopted me? I chose the Graveyard because I was all the way in with my new family.

At school I joined the band under the leadership of the honorable Elijah Brimmer who became a mentor of mine. He showed me tough love, but

---

[1] Through the 1960s the local African-American population referred to the area as "Niggatown." Evidence of the old moniker can be occasionally seen today in the form of "N-Town" graffiti. The name "Black Pearl" was introduced in the 1970s, being derived from the historically majority Black population and the name of "Pearl Street."

Wikipedia

it was exactly what I needed. I loved the band, and music has always been a special part of me. I got plenty of paddles from Mr. Brimmer, as the drum section was considered the bad boys of the school and the most popular. The drum section was like family, but there were two people in particular I became close with. These two had made the decision to chose crime as well, so we came up with a plan to make some real money. One of them lived across the river and knew all the spots where we could rob drug dealers and also get Starter jackets which sold for a hundred a piece, used. The other dude was from Carrollton like me so I knew him well. He was from Niggatown, but it was all love with them and us. He had a cache of weapons and his uncle was the ex-military man that could turn a semi into a fully for 50 bucks. I still had my .38 that I picked up in the burglary and I would soon get another one to match. Our plan had gone well and we were racking up money!

At school, I was beginning to become popular because I wore a different starter jacket everyday, and I had come up on a huge medallion shaped like fire with diamonds on each point.

I eventually got caught in a stolen car and stayed at the Youth Study Detention Center (Youth Study) for a few days before they let me out with conditions from Judge Gray that I would complete a diversion program. I went to a program for a few months that was taught at the Youth Study, but eventually stopped going. Most boys that went to this program ended up in the Youth Study anyway, so I took my chances on the run. The police ended up coming to get me from school because I had a warrant out for my arrest, and I was on my way to doing 18 months at the state run Louisiana Training Institute (LTI), Bridge City. LTI was for kids up to 21 years of age who had longer sentences than the ones at the Youth Center.

The Manufacturing of a Criminal

The one thing I am certain of through my experience is putting a child in jail is always the wrong solution. In most cases a child comes home from prison worse then he was before he went. The penal system is designed to strip you of your dignity and integrity; it awakens a sense of helplessness normal people never experience. As a child this affects the decision making process that has a long term affect, and in many cases a lifetime. I can speak boldly in this arena because the same people that I was in the Youth Study with I met up with them again at Angola less than 10 years later.

The malfunction of the prison system, especially with respect to the youth, is that it creates a network of criminality by caging the children together with no hope, love, or direction for the future. Despite the common goal of rehabilitation, I have yet to find a prison with a success rate in rehabilitation. This signifies to me that rehabilitation does not exist in terms of prisons. I know countless men that have been rehabilitated though, yet all of them will say that rehabilitation comes within the knowledge of oneself.

Prison is basically a grand money scheme developed to replace slavery; a system designed to further oppress the poor, while stimulating the economy of the oppressor. Behind those walls is modern day slavery that can be handed to a child that has made a mischievous mistake. Jail is designed to strip you of your every right, every day, every hour, until you are released. Furthermore, a child in prison becomes a victim of their environment. In other words, an innocent child can become a bully simply because he is afraid of being bullied. Fact.

My first experience being incarcerated was very eventful to say the least. The judge sentenced me to 18 months for the original charge of car theft that I had been placed in Youth Study for. I will never forget the first time knowing I would not be going home, the first time I had been totally secluded from everything that I love, the first time knowing I was in this alone. Aside from the daily oppression from the staff of the institution, I realized there was a certain negative aura among us, for the most part because children were being manufactured as criminals.

The penal system's sole method of operation is fear or the lack thereof. In most jails the every day activity is controlled by the population, which means the strong inmates basically run the jails. A strong inmate can be a guy with a strong physical presence, one whose family is affluent, or even one that keeps himself a mystery, but is not afraid. Also the rats or snitches, dictate the flow of the institution because they keep the authorities in the know with the latest information. These are the observations I made as a child, so I decided to get with the program.

At the Youth Study was a kid called Poppa that for some reason had classified me as weak. He was a chubby kid that talked a lot and was always in some mess. I was a quiet kid, never choosing to make an obstacle of myself. We had had a few words at school one morning, so he had spread the word we would fight. I was terrified.

Although I had had a couple of fights on the street, this was on another level and I was afraid I would get beat up in front of everybody. Poppa and I were in different parts of the jail, and since we went everywhere in units and were escorted by the authorities, I pretty much figured the fight would happen in the mess hall. The mess hall was the cafeteria where we ate, and it had about 12 picnic tables that sat 10 people each. So, in total there were about a hundred kids assembled at chow with a line waiting.

The girls at the Youth Study went to school with us and they had their own table in the mess hall, so this would be the perfect place for a fight. Poppa had been there longer than me, so he had a crew and people cheering him on. As our unit entered the mess hall I spotted Poppa sitting along the wall where we had to pass to get our food. My heart sank to my feet as he stared at me as the line inched closer to him. He was whispering to his friends because talking was not allowed and we only had 10 minutes to eat. Then his counselor notified them their time was up and as Poppa got up to go I was about six feet away. I tensed, waiting for him to run up to me, but he turned around and proceeded to his unit.

The next time I saw Poppa was at the evening meal in the mess hall. There was the same staring and whispering, but the way our units were seated made it almost impossible for him to get to me. This gave me a sense of relief, knowing I would not see him until the next day.

When I got back to my two-man cell that evening all I could do was think about the fight happening tomorrow and what I would do. At eight o'clock we had an option to have TV time and table game recreation. Every unit had their own area, so I didn't have to worry about seeing Poppa. I went to the TV room, but only stared at the screen, oblivious to what was on. All I could think about was tomorrow, and somehow my attitude had changed from one of fear to, "I am ready to do it and get it over with." So, I thought of fighting strategies and ways to make a name for myself because I didn't like the idea of being prey. As I was lost in thought a guy I knew walked up and sat next to me. Normally, we would be playing spades as partners, but not tonight. He told me he had my back and he wasn't gonna let them jump me. This dude's name was T.C. and he was considered strong and from the Melphonine (Melph housing projects). It felt good to know that I had back up. I went back to my cell early that night because I wanted to shadow box before my cellmate came back. As I was working up a sweat throwing punches, thinking of ways to win this fight, I had a bright idea —Strike first. This decision at a young age marked the beginning of a strategy I would use every time danger presented itself.

The next morning at breakfast I was feeling refreshed and ready to get this fight behind me. As I walked in the mess hall I spotted Poppa, but he didn't see me as our unit passed. He looked like he was half asleep and he wasn't paying attention. They served oatmeal that morning and I hated oatmeal. It was then I decided Poppa would wear mine. After I got my plate our unit was to proceed to the table next to Poppa's. Our units were the first two in the room. As everyone else was sitting, I kept walking and by the time Poppa was alerted I was maybe three feet away. He was sitting in the middle of the picnic table so he couldn't just jump up. As he stood I struck him with my plate of food and began to throw my punches, just like I did the night before in my cell. Before Poppa could do anything we were separated and on our way to lock down.

I may have stayed on lock down for a few days, but during this time I began to understand this jail thing. There was a counselor by the name of Brother Al that obviously took a liking to me. Brother Al worked on the night shift, and he was a real cool dude, but he didn't take any shit. He came to my cell the night of the fight once the shift had changed, opened the cell and asked me if I was the one who kicked Poppa's ass? I smirked and nodded, not knowing if I could trust him. He closed the cell and went on his way. Later that night after everyone else was asleep Brother Al opened my door again and gave me all the extra snacks. I was in awe because I didn't even get a snack initially because I was on lock down, and now I had five chocolate chip cookies for myself. Sweet.

After I came back from lock down things were different. It felt as though everyone was watching me. Even the girls were smiling at me when they passed our unit. After I got out of the Youth Study and met up with Poppa at school, he acted as if nothing had happened, and I did the same. From that day on I was considered strong and it was a status I took seriously.

The Youth Study Center was basically a temporary place to stay until you go to court. Most kids that came through there were back at home within a week. Most kids that had to serve time or were on a capital case typically were transferred to the Correctional Youth Center (CYC) which was run like a jail by the city. It was a place that was run by ex-military and wanna-be police. It was common for a deputy to put their hands on you if you got out of line; there was even a deputy who specialized in a roundhouse kick that came from nowhere.

CYC had two dormitories: numbers one and two, and I was in dorm two. Each dorm housed over a hundred boys in bunks stacked three high. I had never seen so many boys in one room until I went to the dorm that night. It was intimidating. The bunks were not assigned, so basically everyone that rocked together, slept together. When I got inside the dorm I set my stuff on an iron table and just sat there trying to find a bed when someone came and guided me to an empty bunk. Of course, I had heard many stories about this dreaded place, but I had no idea what tomorrow would bring.

The sound of a whistle woke me along with loud screaming, "Get up ladies. Rise and shine!" The sound of iron striking iron could be heard as the deputy scraped a billy club up and down the bunks. I watched as every boy scrambled to a painted line parallel to the line of bunks on each side. My neighbor whispered and told me it was 'count time.' The boy on the far end began to count and everyone added a number until it got to the end. Of course, with kids there are bound to be mistakes, especially when we just woke up, but every time we messed up meant more PT or physical training.

PT is how we began every weekday. When I first started it was very hard to keep up, and when you didn't everyone else would rest while you did push ups on the command of the deputy. When it was time for recreation, we went out to the yard, which consisted of a basketball court and huge fences with a razor wire. I remember thinking I had seen this place in the movies, only problem was there were no kids at the place on TV.

I had been at CYC for some months when my friend from school came in my dorm. His name was T.T. and we immediately teamed up. We both were from Carrollton, which made us friends, and we made a vow to stick together. T.T. was kind of a tall skinny kid who was not afraid to speak his mind. His mom and my mom sometimes came together to visit us.

On one particular night the 'strong' in the dorm decided we would have a "Friday night fight" to separate the men from the boys. This happened from time to time, but my name had never been pulled before. The process was simple: if you had a problem with somebody you would call him or her in the back where the cameras couldn't see and you would fight until someone quit. That night somebody picked T.T. and he answered the call. I went to the back to watch his back, and for that somebody called me next and I answered the call as well. The next day there was a lot of talking because the cats we fought were from the Iberville and they had about 15 people in our dorm against me and T.T. We had been trying to get in dorm one because everybody from Carrollton was over there, but it was hard to get into dorm one.

Later one night we went to boxing class because that's where we could talk to our homies in dorm one. It was there that a gang fight broke out. When it was all said and done the deputies had me and T.T. standing on top of the tables with our hands up for hours while everyone else was in bed. That is, until T.T. jumped down and sat. I tried to get him to get back up but he refused. When the deputy came in he began to shout and fuss and tried to get T.T. back on the table, but T.T. refused. More deputies came in and by that time I was off the table too. They grabbed us and dragged us out of the dorm and out of the sight of the rest of the kids. It was in this room they began to punch us and once I saw my boy swing back, I began to fight back too. It was not common for kids to fight back because intimidation was the deputy's' game.

Needless to say, we had many bruises the next day, and it happened to be visitation day! My mom came to see me at least once a month, and she was over due. T.T. had talked to his mom and he was expecting her. They both came. Visitation was behind a glass window, with a telephone to talk. When we showed our moms our bruises, all hell broke loose. Both of our parents' cut up in there, and when they left they called Internal Affairs. That Monday T.T. and I both had attorney visits with child protection and a few days later I was sent back to the Youth Study Center and T.T. was sent to LTI Scotlandville.

Back at the Youth Study Center it was pretty much the same thing. The only thing that had changed was my reputation. It had grown due to the fight with the deputies and that held a lot of weight. My mom kept the pressure on them about the bruises, so I didn't even go on lock down when I arrived. In fact, Brother Al put me back on the unit and he assigned me to a four man cell, which was a privilege. Everything went smoothly until I picked the lock on a window. I never thought in a million years, a paperclip would open a security window, but one night, one did. The counselors would play music for us through the intercom system at night, one of the privileges of being in a quad, so we knew they could not be listening to us. It was when the music was on we would fight if we had something on our chest, or have private conversations.

This window was right above my bed and it was about four feet squared with a thick screen and a tiny lock, like the kind that fit a skeleton key. I had been picking at this lock for more than a week now every night before I went to sleep, and finally one day it opened. I joked about us escaping for a few days, as we would just close the window until night.

One night I put my mattress to the glass, and played like I would break it. One of my mates got up there with me, and just like that, the window came tumbling down. Good thing the music was on and no one heard the loud noise as the four foot glass broke and came tumbling down. Now, the only thing separating us from our freedom was tacked chicken wire. At this point two of us decided to escape, and the other two watched. We quietly placed the glass in my blanket and I kicked the screen off easily. The only problem was we were in the center of four buildings. That meant that there was only one way out and that was to get on the roof. I was the first one through the window, looking for a way up while my boy watched out for me. After seeing all that razor wire just hooked to the roof I thought this was going to be a piece of cake! Eventually two of my comrades managed to get me standing on their shoulders so I could reach for the roof. I struggled to pull myself up as I remembered what I had just told them in the cell a minute ago. "They are going to beat you and treat you like you escaped anyway, so you might as well go." As I made my way to the front side to see if we'd been detected, I smiled because I saw freedom. I told them, "All we have to do is jump down and walk right out of the parking lot."

Now, there's one other thing you should know: every night we had to put our shoes and pants outside our cell door, but we were allowed to keep our sweatshirts. So, on the night we made our escape we converted our sweatshirts to pants by using the sleeves as legs. Imagine four us making our way to St. Bernard Avenue with only socks on our feet and sweatshirts on our legs!

We weren't sure of the time when we actually made it out, but it had to be late because there weren't too many people out. We needed to find a screw driver, so I could hot wire a car. I had told these boys stories that I could steal a car in a minute, which was highly exaggerated.

Nevertheless we found a screw driver; somebody finally gave us one. We were somewhere around Paris Avenue when we came upon a vehicle. I made it look easy and we all climbed in and drove away. I dropped all of them off in their neighborhoods and proceeded to the Graveyard.

I was becoming a legend now and getting a lot of credibility. I had contacts in other areas of the city, which ultimately gave me a network. When I showed up by my boy, Bowlock's mom's house, it was close to daybreak, and Bo let me in through the back door. I slept like a baby for the first time in a long time.

When I walked around in the neighborhood the next day, I felt like a celebrity when I told them I had escaped. I showed up at Fortier High School to see my sis and tell my mom I was okay.

"Momma say turn yourself in before them people kill you," my sister instructed.

"Okay sis," I said.

I walked the halls of Fortier with my chest out, feeling invincible, as I found out my boy who I used to rob with, had been caught and arrested for a robbery that we had done on the west bank. A few days later the police pulled up on me at the Time Saver store on Claiborne and Carrollton. I tried to give them an alias, but that was when I learned at least you had to know the person's birthday you were using as an alias. Back to jail I went, do not pass go, do not collect $200.

When I got back to the Youth Study Center, I was public enemy number one. I was the last one to be captured of the four, and basically it all fell on me. They couldn't send me to CYC because I had a complaint filed against them, so I stayed in solitary confinement for months, but it felt like years. I was then sent to LTI Bridge City because I was to be released within the next year, so they kept me close to home and there was a program my grandfather got me in so I could come home in three months.

It was another system, and by the time I got there I had begun to understand how they operate. Despite a few fights I made it through the program in six months and came home at the age of 17.

At this time, there was an attack on my generation by the government as they dumped guns in our community along with tons of cocaine the government was spreading across the United States. Locally, New Orleans was approaching the title of the being the "murder capital of the world," and violence was becoming the norm. Violence was promoted through the music, police brutality was present, and poverty was the reason. I lived with my mom uptown on Marengo Street, but once I got back to the Graveyard I rarely went home because my mom was all over me. I started hanging with a dude name Applejack, and we would be all over uptown, from the Melph to the Mac to the Calliope (all low income housing projects). We mainly hung in the 12th ward at this time because my best friend Kendall 's mom lived there, until we found out the person responsible for Applejack's Uncle's murder was hanging right under our nose. I didn't even know his uncle, but he was from Carrollton and had migrated to the Calliope and was holding his own. He had been gunned downed in the Calliope for getting too much money in another person's neighborhood.

Applejack wanted to retaliate, so we did. It was the first time I ever shot a rifle, and I had borrowed it from a friend. As we jumped out the two targets separated and ran. I had a clear shot at my target, but the gun didn't shoot. I could hear the shots right around the block: pop,pop,pop! As we ran back to the car I never looked in the direction where I heard the shot. A third person was driving and was panicking at the wheel, the same person who this rifle belonged to. I went crazy about the broken gun and Applejack wanted to kill the driver; I said, "No dude. Chill out!" We made it back to the Graveyard where Applejack told me how he had finished his target, and I couldn't help but to feel like I had failed. Next time, I promised, my gun would shoot. From that moment on I was known for having two revolvers, like a cowboy. I took comfort in knowing there would be no malfunction. The next two years of my life is a book within itself, and has nothing to do with my point—That any child abused for an extended amount of time will likely end up in prison. Once in prison that child will most likely develop into a criminal through a network of acquaintances, and as a result, transition from child criminal to adult criminal by default. The common denominator being the lack of a "Real Man" in their lives; a father. As one reads my story, it can be easily speculated that my mom failed me to some degree; and to those I say, "How dare you." My mother provided me with so much love and nourishment, equipped me with some qualities, which made me the man I am today. My mother was a victim of abuse along with me; she fought for her life many times. My mother raised five children, basically by herself, for that alone she deserves credit. She managed to scrape up the money to pay an attorney when I was running out of time serving a life sentence. My co-defendant, who is innocent, is still in Angola fighting for his life since 1994 because his mom couldn't come up with the money. Same trial, same circumstances, but because he didn't have the money, he ran out of time; FREE DWAYNE WILLIAMS. I will fast forward my story to the morning when Homicide came to my mother's house for me in Gentilly.

Whenever I would want to lay low I would come chill by my mom for a few days. By this time I was snorting heroin and cocaine and had been a part of the havoc that plagued our city at the time. It was January 1995, a time when New Orleans was the murder capital of the world. My life had spun out of control at the age of 20, and the abuse fueled my rage. My careless decisions were the result of me having no respect for God and order, and that was the result of not having a father. Instead I had a man that chose to inflict his frustrations on me, a child in need of direction. My attitude about life was that everything was against me, and my goal was to be respected at all costs. Once I had a taste of that system and the aggressive mentality needed to survive, I quickly added these skills on the street. My boy who I was running with at the time was in jail for attempted murder of a police officer, and the word was our names were being said on the streets, so I decided to lay low. My girlfriend was pregnant with my daughter and she lived by my mom, so I would come home at least once a week to visit.

On this particular day, everyone had left for work and school in the morning except my baby brother who was about 12 at the time. I was suddenly awakened by my little brother who was shaking me and yelling, "The FBI is at the door for you! Wake up!"

I jumped up and saw the unmarked Ford Taurus parked in front of the house. We lived in a two-story single home on the corner of Republic and Lafrenere. From my upstairs window I could see that there were only two police men. I asked my brother, "Did they ask for me?"

"Yes and I told them that you wasn't here," he said.

I went to the other window and saw an escape. Two weeks ago I had helped my mom put up her Christmas decorations, and then take them down. Doing this meant I had to go out of this window, out onto the roof. At the time, I noticed how close the neighbor's house was as I watched their TV while hanging the lights. I sent my brother back downstairs to tell them again, that I wasn't there. He did that and after hearing this, one of the agents walked to the side door of our house. "It was now or never," I thought. I slid out through the window, climbed to the roof and jumped with all my might into the neighbor's yard and rolled, just like in the movies. Quickly, I walked out of the neighbors yard and onto the sidewalk, never looking back. The detectives were behind me and all I needed to do was make it to the corner, so I could run for my life! I got away from the house that day, but it was clear the police were out looking for me.

The same unmarked car had been seen in the Graveyard, in Niggatown, and by my boy's momma's house—the guy who was already in jail. I had no choice but leave Carrollton, so my friend, Dookey, offered to let me stay with him until I figured out what to do next.

Dookey lived in the ninth ward on Mazant, so no one could find me there. I would lie on the backseat of Dookey's Cadillac as we drove through Carrollton trying to figure out what the police wanted me for. Dookey was about 10 years older than me and he had a heroin habit. He always made me promise never to shoot anything in my vein, and I never did because that same year Dookey died of an overdose.

It turns out I was a suspect in a murder case. Even though I was on the run for murder, I didn't take it seriously because I felt invincible. It was common for me to pop up in the Graveyard or Niggatown during the day even though I knew the police were looking for me.

It all ended one night at a bar called Simmons at about two a.m. My boy Bowlock had picked me up that night and our first stop was a bar called Detour on Martin Luther King Boulevard. It began to get late and my boy was ready to go, but I had bumped into my chick so I was trying to line something up. She wanted me to meet her at Simmons because she and her girl were going there. Bowlock agreed to go and we paid to get in the bar. Immediately, I saw a police man who knew me, but I was positive he didn't get a look at me because I had had my hood on.

At the time, I was selling nickel and dime bags of weed to get some money and as soon as we walked in, a guy wanted to buy some. I told the person to follow me outside, not knowing that the police were waiting for me there. As I stepped outside I could see that there were police present and their attention was focused on me. I tried to walk up to Claiborne against traffic and noticed a car on the corner waiting for me. I looked back and the police were closing in; I had nowhere to run, so I raised my hands in surrender and asked what did I do? They asked for my name and birthday, so I gave them my alias—my brother-in-law's name and birthday. Unfortunately for me, they already knew who I was.

Orleans Parish Prison

In 1995 Orleans Parish Prison (OPP) was complete hell. From the horrible living conditions to the treatment by the deputies, the way that this place operated was torture. There were more people than bunks, which meant there were people sleeping on the floor all while water dripped from the leaky pipes in the ceiling. There already were close to a hundred guys in my assigned dormitory as I searched for a dry spot on the floor to lay my mattress. I stretched out on that hard mattress and wondered how I was going to get myself out of this one.

After a few court dates and plenty of fights, I realized that I wasn't going home and someone from my neighborhood was testifying against me for a murder that happened in my neighborhood. After more court dates and many more fights I was convicted in less than a year for First Degree Murder.

A few months later I was at my sentencing praying that the jury would decide to give me life instead of the death penalty, as my mom, pastor, and my daughter's mom pleaded with the jury to spare my life. The jury decided on a life sentence and I was to serve the remaining of my life at Angola.

Once I was sentenced I went to my God in prayer understanding that it was in his hands. My fellow inmates saw that I was sharing the word with others, as my pastor would keep me with material. Some inmates took that as a weakness. One night when they had an open floor fight someone that was fairly new wanted to fight me. I refused to fight until he touched me first. He threw a punch.

We began to fight and he soon realized that I wasn't the weak one, as I knocked him down time after time. Then all of his friends jumped me and beat me up pretty badly. It was days before I could open my jaw because it had been fractured, but I stayed there and defended myself until I was sent to Angola.

Up the River

I will never forget that long miserable ride to the Louisiana State Prison at Angola, distance aside; it was the longest ride I had ever taken. As you ride those miles with another, chained to your side, you can't help but feel as if this is a one way ticket, no return possible. As I played back the events that brought me there I felt regretful, but not yet remorseful.

It was then that I reflected on a scripture reading I had learned in church as a child, "the Lord will not put more on you than you can bear." I took that with me on the ride that changed my life.

As we approached Angola I was instantly intimidated by the size of this plantation sitting on top of a hill. We entered the gate and I realized I was in a whole different world. The crazy thing is that we were a chain gang of about 30 young men, most under the age of 25, and going through the administration process at Angola in the same building that held the death row inmates and the Correctional Officers (CO) who would use them as trophies. There, you get stripped of your name and are issued a number, which becomes your primary identification; 334377 is mine. I know it better than my social security number. We took a quick ride on the bus from the front gate to the 'A' Building where we met the political prisoners, or coons, to further intimidate you and influence your thinking.

I had been incarcerated since I was 13, but this shit was on a whole different level. I was 21 at this time, but I had never experienced fear like this before. Imagine a walkway with fences on both sides that are as long as the eye can see. Along those sides are real live convicts who are at "recreation" when a line of "fresh meat" comes through. As I took my first walk to the cell block that would be my home, I heard the convicts yelling; and they are allowed to say whatever they want. They're picking out the guys who would be their 'ho.' A ho is a male that has been forced to be a sex slave of a convict.

They split up the new convicts, and I ended up in C block, which was medium security. When I finally got a chance to go out to the yard I went straight for the basketball court. My co-defendant had arrived before me, but he was in minimum security, which happened to be across the fence. I would see people standing and talking at the fence, but I would mind my own business. Sometime during that first week I was shooting a ball when I was told that somebody wanted me at the fence. It was Wayne, my co-defendant. He said I needed to get out of C block because it was the weak block, or the "ho" block. In laymen terms, it was the cell block that housed homosexuals that were running from their slave masters, dudes that were running from pressure, or the young dudes 16-21 that were just coming to Angola. One can get a bad reputation in that block he said, and that's all I needed to hear.

The next week we started to work. This was the worse week of my life. As we walked miles to and from work in brand new jeans and boots, I got rashes between my legs and blisters on my feet, but I continued to work. I was in a cell with an old man named Understanding. Yes, that was really his name. He took a hand full of pills every evening with coffee that he would heat up by burning paper and heating a coke can full of coffee—Clearly against the rules. What bothered me was that he didn't work because of medical reasons and he stayed in our two-man cell all day. When I came in one day he had cleaned the cell, and had a sheet wrapped around him like a skirt. When I walked in the cell I didn't say anything, pulled my locker box out and sat close to the bars to catch the news. He sat on his bed and took his pills, crossed his legs and drank his coffee. I got up to use the bathroom, which caused him to slide down to the end of his bed as I turned my back to him to urinate. Already bothered, but not certain that I was being disrespected; I noticed that he didn't have boxers on under the sheet. This caused me to get angry.

As they were delivering our last meal of the day, I had decided to strike; this was my chance to increase my reputation and get moved from C block. I struck as I saw the first Inmate pass our cell with the food because I knew the CO was close behind. I had sized up Understanding and I knew he wouldn't be a match, especially when he was on pills and wouldn't see it coming. I landed the first lick on his mouth. He didn't jump up as I wanted him to, but fell back in defense. He was between bunks as I swung blows while he tried to ball up to protect himself. By this time the convicts had crowded in front of our cell, which caused that CO to come. The deputies stormed in and cuffed me and brought me to the dungeon, which was where you waited to go to disciplinary court.

I was sentenced to eight days of extra duty and transferred to 'A' block. As I waited weeks in the dungeon for the transfer I learned all types of things that were going on all over the prison. I learned all about the 'out camps' and how they all had their own cell block and extended lock down plus how convicts moved around the prison on their own terms. When I got to 'A' block it was a completely different atmosphere. There were poker games, real full court basketball games, gambling tickets, and men in real relationships. I basically learned many lessons as I went five months without a write-up and made the board to go down the walk, which meant minimum security.

The difference between medium and minimum security is two-man cells versus a dormitory of 120 and the freedom to move around and do something constructive. I was assigned to the dormitory Pine 4 and to the bed next to a guy named Jerome Morgan, who immediately became my friend. We ate together and shared in each other's quest for freedom. There was something different about Jay, and we had a common goal. We filled out our law library request on the same dates so we could help each other in the law library, and we both played sports. There was also the prison 'Club' scene which was very political, I must say, but it was there that I met Robert Jones.

Robert was appointed "Inmate Counsel," meaning he had a paralegal degree and the prison hired him to work with other prisoners. I would always see him in the law library, and I finally officially met him at an event that his 'club' was hosting. Robert was the president of his 'club.'

In 1997 the warden, Burl Cain decided to shake up the population of the West Yard, which meant I was moved to 'Oak 4.' My boy, Jay was moved to 'Camp C.'

Oak 4 was laid back, full of convicts that basically obeyed the rules and were rewarded with jobs. I did 90 days and put in for a job in the kitchen. I had somebody pulling strings for me. I started to pay attention to a guy name Goldie, whose real name was Alfred Carter. He caught my attention because he was always discussing the law and he seemed to know what he was talking about. The word was that he was given a life sentence back in the 1980's for distribution of heroin, and was busted again for the same thing with a fresh life sentence. It was common to get a jail house lawyer to work on your case for a fee of $500, and when I approached Goldie with the proposition, he said he was too busy with his own case. He told me that, "Nobody knows your case like you. Don't trust nobody with your freedom." Despite being busy, he agreed to help me and introduced me to the Criminal Code of Procedure and told me to write down everything that I thought went wrong in my trial. This laid the foundation for my appeal, and every evening I would work on my case in the game room.

Also in Oak 4 I was amazed to learn that they had a tackle football team. I played, so I went to try out. I had heard that you could move around the whole prison playing sports which is was key because I had been trying to get in touch with my co-defendant concerning our case. I had found some interesting documents in the DA file that had come in, thanks to my mom. Of course, football practice (I made the team) took time away from me going to the law library and Goldie quickly took notice and informed me that the Anti Terrorist Bill time limitations were in full affect, and the courts didn't care how well you could catch that football!

I continued to play, but I made sure to make all of my appointments with the law library. Goldie had a dude called Freddie Mc Zeal who was sharp with the law too, so we all planned to go to the law library one evening as I had been denied on direct appeal and was preparing for post conviction relief. There was a list of guys who were approved to go to the law library every day, but the 'Captain' on each shift could give 10 additional passes to others.

On this particular day we got there so late that the 'Captain' had already assigned his maximum of 10 passes. As usual we proceeded to the gate, but our passes were forged with the 'Captain's' signature. We had been getting away with this for months. So, we entered the law library as usual and started researching. I was learning how to shepardize[2] a case and find more cases applicable to mine.

At 'count time,' the 'Captain' called out Goldie's name, my name, and our friend, Freddy's name. We'd been found out, written up as "a threat to security" and sent back to the cell blocks.

Back in medium security we had limited access to legal aid, which made it more difficult to file my post conviction. They sent me and Goldie to 'A' block while Freddy went to Raven, a cell block at Camp D. Goldie continued to help me with my case until he was sent to Camp C, and I to the main prison. It was there I met Michael Therriot who I paid to take all of the information that I had compiled and file my post conviction relief to the District Court. This was in 1997. I got a denial from the court in 1998.

I quickly went back to the drawing board trying to find something that I had missed. I submitted another appeal to the Fourth Circuit in 1999, but was denied again in 2000. I had one appeal left for the state, and I was beginning to panic. I was aware of the one year time limit for the federal court that was running simultaneously with the three year state time limit. That's when I learned from Goldie that to preserve your year

---

[2] Case law is based upon precedent or authority. In order to find out if a case can be used as authority, check to see whether the case has been followed, distinguished, limited or questioned in subsequent court cases. This is done by "Shepardizing" – using Shepard's Citations to see how and when another court has cited the first decision. Shepardizing a case helps determine the precedential value of a legal authority. It is crucial to make sure the precedents are up-to-date.

University of Delaware Library

in the Federal court you must always keep something in the works in court. This was critical because your year in federal court represented your last shot! As I prepared for my writ to the Louisiana Supreme Court, I was confident in my abilities to do it all on my own. I focused on the opinions of the judges from the Fourth Circuit, and submitted my petition, praying that they would have mercy on me.

In these times I was praying more, asking God to stand on his word. I was talking to my mom on the phone, but I tried to call no more than twice a month because the cost of calls were so high. I told her that I needed a lawyer because I was running out of time and options. She told me that she was expecting some money and would get the lawyer for me. Kevin Boshea was a hot appellate attorney at the time and my mom hired him in 2001. He withdrew the writ that I submitted, and informed the court that he was my counsel of record. He re-filed my post conviction relief to the Louisiana Supreme Court and I was granted a hearing to determine whether the newly discovered evidence was in fact Brady material[3]. Unfortunately, the trial Judge, Leon Cannizzaro, determined that it was not and denied the petition.

We appealed Cannizzaro's decision and opinion to the Fourth Circuit Court of Appeals and I was finally granted a new trial in 2003. I opted not to face a vicious prosecution a second time and pled guilty to manslaughter and was released in 2003.

New World Order

During my time at Angola, since I had a life sentence it was hard for me to learn any type of trade because they kept those limited spots for

---

[3] The Brady Rule, named after Brady v. Maryland, 373 U.S. 83 (1963), requires prosecutors to disclose materially exculpatory evidence in the government's possession to the defense. A "Brady material" or evidence the prosecutor is required to disclose under this rule includes any evidence favorable to the accused--evidence that goes towards negating a defendant's guilt, that would reduce a defendant's potential sentence, or evidence going to the credibility of a witness.

Legal Information Institute [LII]

people who had short prison terms. When I was released, I was 29 years old with a GED and no work experience. I know this is when people say that recidivism is a choice, but I challenge them to find a job as a third class citizen. In 2003 my brother-in-law helped me get a job at Security, a moving company that would pack and move you for a lot of money. I started out as a mover and after about five months the supervisor ask me if I wanted to be promoted to lead packer, which meant I had more responsibility. I said, "Yes." What I didn't know was that this meant was going through a federal background check for permission to drive a company vehicle. The end result was me getting fired for lying on my application.

As I struggled with my transition into society, I had no direction, no help, and no encouragement. I wanted to do the right thing. My mother was my only means of support and she tried to keep some money in my pocket. Yet I refused to sit at home and watch my mom work two and three jobs as I stayed at home and played the game with my brother. I ran in to some dudes I knew that were getting mad cash making fake checks and ID's. I hooked up with them and made some easy money on the coast and after a few months shit was looking good. I had taken the money and started a business, Kas N Daniel, a food delivery and catering service. This was in 2004.

We, my girlfriend, Chelbi and I, went to Miami that year because we now had money and it was fun being able to buy whatever I wanted. Chelbi was pregnant at the time, so I bought a ton of stuff for the baby, so much so that we had no room in the car on the way back. When we got home I had more fake checks that I hadn't used and decided to take a trip to Gonzales, an outlet mall, and buy some more stuff. I had my pregnant girlfriend with me, and in the end, we both went to jail for identity theft.

I had had about three years left on parole, so I knew this was goodbye for me. I ended up doing five years on a 10 year sentence, and I was released in 2010.

The Plan

When I came home in 2010 I had a different outlook on life, and I learned a trade while incarcerated for those last five years—Cutting hair. At the beginning of the incarceration I was sent to Richwood Correctional Center. The warden of the jail's name was Tillory and I knew him from Angola. He was a Major at Angola and his wife worked in the infirmary. He was a black man. When I told him who I was he gave me a job as the barber for the entire jail, which meant I was responsible for delivering and picking up equipment from each dorm, as well as providing maintenance and sterilization. As the head barber I was also responsible for cutting Warden Tillory's hair at least once a week and he demanded that I shaved him with a straight razor every time. I had never used a straight razor until that first day he pulled it from his desk. I remember shaking as I edged under the wardens neck, not familiar with the free-hand stroke or the reverse and not understanding how to stretch the skin to prevent from cutting. I managed to pull it off without a scratch. I stayed there for a few years until I was sent to Elayn Hunt Correctional Center (EHCC), where I also got a barber job on the compound.

Although I worked a few construction jobs for the first year or so when I came home in 2010, I always had cutting hair on my mind. One day I went to talk to Big Wayne, a friend from Carrollton, about getting in his barber shop and he agreed. That same day I cut a boy's hair, but his mom went crazy because she wasn't satisfied with the haircut. Big Wayne fixed the haircut and told me that I wasn't ready to cut hair in a shop.

A few weeks later my mom sent me to my cousin's barbershop, Impressive, to speak with Mo about working there. His real name was Maurice Isles and he was about the same age as my mom. He had been cutting hair since he was a boy and his father was a barber too. This man taught me everything about barbering, as well as the importance of being a part of the community as a business. I worked there under his license until I got my own. As a matter of fact, I was working there one day as the news came on, when suddenly they said a name that caught my attention. I looked at the TV and saw that my friend from Angola, Jerome Morgan, had been released. I told everyone to quiet down as I learned that Jay had been released on bond.

A few months passed as I asked around if anyone had seen him, when someone came to get a haircut that had seen Jay and gave me his number. As I cut his hair he told me Jay was on an ankle monitor and that's why he hadn't been out much. Later that day I made my way to Pontchartrain Park to see my friend. We caught up and I told him that I was cutting hair in the sixth ward, and he told me he was cutting hair at home.

One day Jay came to the shop to visit me and he wondered if he could get a chair in the shop where I worked. I told him I didn't think it was a good move, but I was thinking about starting my own shop and that he could work under my license. Weeks later Jay said that he found a space for us and I went with him to see it. He brought me to the Resurrection After Exoneration (RAE) building and I told him it would work. In less than a month we opened the doors of RAE Grooming Barbershop, which later became the Real Gentlemen Barbershop. As Jerome's case reached its end another friend of ours was released, Robert Jones. Robert Jones quickly became the third team member as we all had a common goal, and that was to mentor youth.

Jerome and I had already drafted our mentoring program with the help of Kelly Orians and Rising Foundations. We won first place in NOLA's Pitch Competition sponsored by Propeller, by presenting our program as an economic solution for the educational crisis in New Orleans. At first, Robert Jones played in the background, as he feared the D.A. would try to use anything against him, so he distanced himself from us as we privately formulated the platform for Free-Dem Foundations. Robert Jones was the missing piece to the puzzle. While Jerome brought social justice and humanitarian ideals, I considered myself a businessman and an organizer. Robert brought a political and economical aspect to our team, which ultimately sealed the cracks.

Together we form a team of knowledge and experience capable of reaching any youth. We used this platform to mentor youth and speak at various schools.

The three of us were watching the news when a segment came on about a mother whose son had fallen into the wrong crowd after his father was gunned down. The kid had just reached puberty. We listened to this mother's plea as her son was sentenced to 66 years for robbery. Her main concern was that too many times our youth slip through the cracks, and somebody had to do something to prevent this. This woman's story touched us all and prompted us to write this book. It is my dream that this book reaches the hands of a young person who need inspiration. To them I say, "You can! As you go through life's ups and downs do not ever decide to do something wrong, because it is then you decide to fail."

I pray a single mother looking for her mate reads my story; to you I say, "Be intuitively careful of the men you bring around your children. I empathize with you, but understand the wrong man can have a long term affect on your child, even if it's only through neglect."

I also hope that the single mom struggling to control a son in puberty thumbs through these pages, and hears first hand of the penal system and how it is designed to make a child into a criminal. In any event, these words were written in an effort to help that child who has been given up on and is ultimately a victim of circumstance. I encourage that mother whose knees are hurting from praying. There are real men out here who want to help; and our resolve is unbreakable.

—Daniel Rideau

Jerome's Story

Know Thyself

My first socialization with others outside the home was at the community park, the community primary school, and the community church all at the same time. In proximity, the church was across the street from the school, and the park was across the street from the church. The foster home I was placed in on September 30, 1979, was also across the street from the school, but on the opposite side of the block, down the street and in the next block. I was there between the years 1979-1991. Back then, Pontchartrain Park was a glorious neighborhood with a culture of ownership, self-dignity and role models within the home. It was common for several generations to reside in the same house, or many family members moved out of the same dwelling, but remained in the neighborhood all their lives, or lived close by. This close-knit community has a very rich history that produced many noble residents, such as mayors, district attorneys, the Environmental Protection Agency (EPA) Administrator under former President Obama, actors, jazz musicians and the first Black Supreme Court Chief Justice in Louisiana, just to name a few in recent times. As a matter of fact, in 1955 as an outgrowth of the "separate but equal" doctrine, Pontchartrain Park was the first suburban-style subdivision developed "by" and "for" middle-class African Americans during racial segregation in Louisiana, after the disenfranchisement of the reconstruction period.

At the time it was built, segregation of public (state-sponsored) schools was declared unconstitutional by the Supreme Court of the United States in 1954 in Brown v. Board of Education. This was much before the remaining Jim Crow laws were overruled by the Civil Rights Act of 1964 and the Voting Rights Act of 1965. Nonetheless, this black neighborhood has always maintained 98 percent home-ownership and prominent respect despite not having civil rights or voting rights during the time this neighborhood was established. Albeit, none of these local historical facts were taught to me at all during those most impressionable years—Not at school, church, the park or home.

At the center of the neighborhood is the approximately a 183-acre, amoeba-shaped Pontchartrain Park. It was built by the legend in golf course architecture and construction, Joseph M. Bartholomew, Sr. It originally opened as the Pontchartrain Golf Course in 1956. The course was renovated in 1979 and renamed after him to honor the first African American inducted into the Greater New Orleans Sports Hall of Fame. Two curvilinear roads wrap around the park and serve as the primary neighborhood passageways. Smaller movement of interior streets, and un-obvious shortcuts, create a twisting pattern that stands in contrast to how other neighborhoods are developed like a grid.

Southern University at New Orleans (SUNO), a historically black university, opened a campus in the northwest corner of Pontchartrain Park in 1959. Across the street was a stadium named after the New Orleans African American baseball legend, Wesley Barrow, in 1957, who influenced hundreds, if not thousands, of young men and players, both locally and nationally. Wesley Barrow had a 40-plus year career in America's favorite pastime as a player and manager for numerous local African American sandlot, semi-pro and professional teams during the era of baseball segregation and beyond.

The stadium sits on the park's northernmost point. Right across the railroad tracks you'll find a large body of water known as Lake Pontchartrain. As adolescents, we would sneak out and walk to the lake's beach front and swim there during those humid months, even though the water was always said to be polluted.

The foster home mentioned earlier, was a one story, half brick structure, with five bedrooms, a living room, a large den, one full bathroom, and one half-bathroom. There were also two sizable sheds in the back yard. One was used as the laundry room, and the bigger shed stored hardware, tools and lawn mowers. I always remember the fig tree that was planted in the backyard, which grew to be much taller than I was during those childhood years.

The front yard was adorned with a curvy multi-colored, tiled walkway, a stone bench and a black lamp post. The house was on the very first street once you get into the neighborhood. I lived there with my elder brother of three years, my younger sister of 19 months, and three other foster siblings, who all were older than I was by at least two years.

All the males slept in the same room, next to the foster parent's room. My foster parents also slept in separate bedrooms right next to each other. The female's bedrooms were the most recent expansions to the back part of the home. The fostered female's bedroom was next to our foster parent's biological daughter's bedroom. She had to be 28 years old back then, working at a department store, and attending college classes to become a teacher. My foster parent's older son, and only other biological child, lived in the upper ninth ward. He served time in the military, and drove chartered buses during those days. He, himself, had a daughter maybe four years older than I was, and a son younger than I was by only months. The foster parents' kids would all visit or sleep over quite often throughout my upbringing. Besides their grandson, my sister and I were the youngest.

For some strange reason, it was known from day one that the other siblings at the foster home were favored over my siblings and I. My guess would be that it was because they were there before us. My mama (as I referred to my foster mom) was a 54 year-old retired department store sales clerk. Paw Paw, her husband, was three years her senior and had worked at the SUNO bookstore since a couple years after he purchased the home in 1957.

Actually, the favoritism in the home was mostly displayed by the special relationship between Paw Paw and the youngest of the other siblings. The ages of the other siblings were nine, six and five—The lone male being the middle child who was only a couple weeks younger than my biological brother. We were a close-in-age group of boy roommates. My younger sister, on the other hand, was four years younger than the youngest of the other two girls. Our other foster sister was older by seven years than my sister and six years older than I was. I was only three years old when we arrived.

"The Park," as we so affectionately referred to our neighborhood, was a place where I felt safe. The neighbors were neighbors, an extension of the family by way of being a child growing up in the neighborhood.

I made friends very quickly. I made friends next door, across the street, down the street on both ends, and on either end of the total area of one square mile. Most of my friends' families were so genuinely welcoming when I would be invited to their homes. There was one family only four houses down from where I stayed that would host parties regularly for every holiday of the year, plus special occasions such as birthdays, graduations, and marriages. It didn't too much matter the occasion, it was a neighborhood affair.

Pontchartrain Park was also a part of "NORD" (New Orleans Recreation Department). Therefore, physical activities, camaraderie, fairness, respect, teamwork and competitive thinking were always available through organized sports, almost all year-round. My favorite sport was football, then basketball. I really enjoyed playing and watching both these team sports. I did like to play baseball, but I didn't enjoy spectating. Pontchartrain Park had a very prideful reputation. We were

Patriots! Our playground nickname was the black rendition of the 1980 New England Patriots' NFL team logo. Our opponents were area parks within what was called the "Lakeshore Division." We would host or go to neighboring parks like Joe Brown, Milne, Gorretti, Kenilworth, Delgado, Digby, and Willie Hall to play football games or scrimmage.

Pontchartrain Park also had a grown man's softball league, which would play against these same neighboring parks that almost everybody and their mama used to go to many nights during the spring, summer, and fall months. During the games, the children played basketball, touch football (or pitch-up tackle), and/or be on the park playground swinging, sliding, climbing the monkey bars, eating popcorn, nachos with cheese and jalapeño peppers, cold drinks, potato chips, and hot dogs sold from the park's concession stand. As a child, I was so small in stature, my neighborhood friends would tease me about possibly growing up to be a midget. Oh yes, I may have appeared small in stature, but that just motivated me more to show myself as a huge person on the inside.

The Mary Dora Coghill Elementary School of today is not located in the same neighborhood it was when I had the privilege of attending there from kindergarten in 1980/81, then graduating from sixth grade in 1987. Make no mistake, as I know, the school now in Gentilly Woods is an exceptional one. It has the highest enrollment of any school of its kind. Nonetheless, that school, actually being located in Pontchartrain Park, was a very big deal to the history of the neighborhood. As the center of the community, the primary school also became central to our lives. Thus, it followed that anything central to us as a community was never physically outside of the circle. "As it is in Heaven, give us this day."

In kindergarten class, I remember talking to a female classmate sitting next to me at a line of long tables, with children sitting on both sides. She lived in a corner house, two blocks down, on the furthest end of the block. To my recollection, our verbal exchange at age five was quite pleasant. We only broke our acquaintance because it was "water break time." Those who wanted water had to make a uniform line. Looking back at it now, I probably took every opportunity, at age five, to get up from the table. I can't remember if I rushed to the water fountain (like it's so second nature to do as a child) or not. Whatever the reason, my next door neighbor punched me, dead square in my nose as I turned around to return to my seat. My eyes watered, and my nose bled. I don't remember what happened after that, but apparently the educators resolved the incident with care. After that, my next door neighbor and I fought again on three or four more separate occasions, for varied reasons during those days of growing up as "ride or die" friends.

Real talk—He was one of my best friends. We stood together when either one of us were outnumbered, as was the code that was established with all of my closest friends.

I had fights with plenty of my boyhood friends growing up. That's just how we settled our differences as young males. From the fifth year of the "birth to puberty" stage of life, we learned the meaning of "respect" in the physical sense, whether you win, lose or draw in a street fight. The very next day, or sometimes later that same day, we would be back playing sports in the street, in the schoolyard after school, at the park playing "it," hide-n-go seek, or cool cans. As we grew those activities became house parties, school dances, team sport games, or going to each other's house. My foster parents didn't like my friends coming over too often, so more times than not, we were at their homes playing Atari, Nintendo and Sega, He-Man, G. I. Joe and Legos.

We may "get it off our chest" more often than not during our practice of conflict resolution amongst ourselves. However, you have got to understand, it makes a pivotal difference to have other young males and older men as tangible examples of how to cultivate our masculine aggression into respectable support amongst your peers, or generation, and paying those principles forward with the "gentle touch of nature." Which brings to mind a message I received on the very day I wrote this part of my story on one of my social media profiles:

February 6th, 9:28 a.m.

Friend: "I don't know if you remember me, but I'm glad to see you home."

Jerome: "Thanks! Please refresh my memory? My apologies."

Friend: "We used to attend camp at Coghill, and my grandparents used to stay across the street. I used to spend my summers on Mithra. She used to grow the hot peppers in the front yard."

Jerome: "Come by the shop some time."

Friend: "I was from the CTC (A'Cross the Industrial Canal) and would have to go to camp in Gentilly. You stood up for me during a fight after camp. You lived around there, but I didn't. I never forgot that because one of the guys stopped wanting to fight me in to our teenage years because of that day.

Even when we got older I used to bring my people from the CTC to the park to play. Dudes just knew that I knew you and a few other guys from Gentilly."

The "gentle touch of nature" is what the Honorable Marcus Garvey described as "...no written law compelling other races to stand together. They are brought together by the gentle touch of nature. The unwritten law of nature causes them to stand together on all occasions. So wheresoever you'll find them in the fields, that one gentle touch of nature causes them to stand together. If need be, die together." Within the perimeters of my neighborhood, we had that affection. Within the walls of my foster family, we didn't.

In elementary school I began tutoring fellow students and getting involved with a lot of basic, creative, educationally inspiring activities. I helped paint the hallway's concrete walls with different life forms of nature in their natural habitat, like a school of sharks in water, for example. I did a lot of the drawing for a six foot by four foot Black History mural and colored the images with mosaic-like tiles made from small square cut-outs from construction paper. It was gorgeous! So much so, we took a field trip to Atlanta to present it to the Reverend Dr. Martin Luther King, Jr. Center in honor of his great legacy as our expression of commemorative art.

Sometime around 1985, I was chosen to appear on "Kid's Break," a channel 38 after school news segment. My topic was dinosaurs. My last three elementary school years, from fourth grade til sixth (1985-1988), was filled with moments just like that to remember.

In the fourth grade, three of my friends and I decided that we would participate in the school's annual "Putting On The Lips" talent show contest. Our performance would be a lip-syncing rendition of New Edition's "Lost In Love." The contest was the school's version of the popular 80's TV show called, "Putting On The Hits." It was a lip-syncing contest, so contestants had to be on point with their "non-vocal" talents. With the songs we used, we imitated the image and choreography of the singing group to showcase our talent. I don't think we placed in the competition the school year of 1985-1986. I don't remember practicing much for the contest that year.

The next year we learned from our previous failure, and with a couple different members, performed New Edition's "Earth Angel." We blew everyone's mind, and placed first. The only friend in the group that didn't live in Pontchartrain Park had a beautiful mom, and aunts, who committed to being our choreographers and dressed us to impress and compete in the contest. We practiced religiously every day after school at my friend's house who lived in Press Park.

My sixth grade year, and the third year we participated in the school's annual talent show, we were not allowed to compete. The principal wanted to give others a fair opportunity to win, so she asked us to be the contest's featured performance who would perform after the contestants. Of course, we wanted to be fair, so, indeed, we agreed.

We had to replace one group member, Derrick "Deke" Remble, who didn't want to participate anymore. I think, because he was so embarrassed about being 13 years old in the sixth grade (and, yes, he did graduate that same year, with the rest of us.) However, he did make sure that our friend, who lived two houses down from where I lived, could be his replacement.

Our choreographer, who was still my Press Park friend's mom, hid us in the kitchen part of the cafeteria during the talent show. The cafeteria was always converted into an auditorium whenever need arose for an inside event.

It was a challenge because this friend had little to no rhythm. Despite that, we received a request to perform at SUNO. We would conduct practices by his house, on our own, with additional practice time to also perform "Before You Turn On The Lights," by the World Class Wrecking Cru, featuring Michel'le. My Press Park friend's cousin was our Michel'le. It was so fulfilling to have the experience, or what should be called the expertise, to reap the benefits of your performance as a reflection of how committed you are to the preparation. It definitely taught me that the journey "is" the success, not the destination. But, before I get too far ahead of myself, let's get back to the school's kitchen.

We stood out of sight that entire evening until it was time for us to take the stage. You should have seen the moment of surprise that greeted us which was quickly followed by applause.

We were dressed in traditional tuxedos with tails, white shirts, black bow ties and cummerbunds. My friends all wore black tuxes, while I wore a white one because, as in previous years, I was the lead "lip-sync-er."

We took the stage in a position with our backs to the audience waiting for the music to start. Then, as the Deele's "Two Occasions" began, we turned around, one by one, precisely in rhythm with the song (just like all of the great guy groups did in those days and before). The crowd went into a frenzy.

It's not even possible to formulate any group of verbiage to accurately express the level of elation that came from all the hardships up to that point. And, not all hardships are unwanted. Think about wanting tightly toned muscles. You have to workout to get them to form. So, the challenges to get to that destination should be welcomed. So, in that spirit, I embrace hardship because I'm headed into the destination of having a brain muscle, and heart muscle, to be just as intelligent and compassionately formed as anyone else's.

By the end of summer 1987, I was enrolled in a seventh ward public junior high school. The closest public junior high schools in Pontchartrain Park's district were either in the eighth ward or New Orleans' East (locally referred to as 'the East'). Neither school had as good of a reputation for success as the seventh ward public school. Nevertheless, it was outside of my school district, so I had to get a GPA permit to allow me to be registered as a student there. At that juncture, I was encouraged to decide for myself, what school would seem most interesting to me. I liked the idea of going to the seventh ward school because my foster sister, right above me in age, attended there. Although she was moving on to a selective admission high school in seventh ward, New Orleans for her freshman year. It was a historically Black college preparatory high school, established back in 1917. The history of this junior high school I desired to attend was not as significant, but its cool reputation was something that I gravitated towards.

During those most impressionable years of human life, I was always active in church, at the least, every Sunday morning. I participated in the holiday plays, and assumed all the duties of a child during those church-clothes and penny-loafer days. What I remember most was the church project I was able to do using "Play-Dough." With the clay, I replicated the legend, Jesse Owens, adorned with the four gold medals he'd received in Berlin, Germany for track and field. I positioned him on top of the medal stand, arms raised, with the other medalists sandwiching him in the moment. I depicted one of those guys as white, and the other Asian. I'm sure that wasn't the ethnicity of those individuals, but it was important to me to include the three most populous ethnicities of the human race.

Ready or not, adolescence was quickly approaching. Once that first wet dream arrived, my perspective changed like a Baptized person arising out of the water, a born-again creature. I went from having one girl of my interest, not being open to tongue-kissing, leaving in disgust when I caught my foster brother watching a guy performing oral sex on a female on the Playboy channel, and just being a rumbling-tumbling boy, to having many girls of my interest, not being against tongue-kissing anymore, pursuing sexual relations with the females and just overall discovering my male hood. I think "male hood" is a more accurate term than "manhood" because the term "man" can actually mean male or female.

Although the stages of life are not gender specific: Birth-Puberty-Adulthood-Marriage-Parenthood-Elderhood-Mortality-Afterlife, the way human beings naturally develop (no matter their sexual preference) becomes distinctly different during the phases of adolescence and procreation, depending on gender.

There was never any moments, throughout my time growing up in the household foster care provided for me, that my foster dad spent any significant time with his foster sons outside of the one road trip we took to Daly City, CA to visit their biological son, in the brand new late 80's beige Dodge family van. Of course, I learned a lot about my potential in being a male adult, parent and elder just from having an elder male parent in the household. However, it's really difficult to explain the dynamics of Paw Paw's presence in the household because he showed absolutely no gesture of affection to anyone but my foster sister who was right above me in age.

I used to think he hated my brother Harry because he would have the worst reactions towards him whenever he did something wrong. My foster brother would be treated with controllable disgust from Paw Paw at times as well. I, on the other hand, was never disciplined by him at all, based on my recollection. The masculine gestures of affection that guided me, in those early years, mostly came from males outside of the household, but well within the community. Paw Paw was not a hateful guy, just one who didn't seem too fond of raising other people's children, I guess. Nevertheless, my foster mom did spend time with us attending church services every Sunday, parades every carnival season and vacationing every summer to places outside of Louisiana.

The last summer vacation we went on, as a family was a ten day east coast bus tour. It was organized by the card club she was a member of, which consisted of a bunch of elderly women who would take turns hosting games at their homes every so often. The card games by our house were always fun, and packed with women who were always willing to spare some good advice. "... Go play with your brothers, handsome. It's not good for you to be hangin' 'round a bunch of women, okay."

On this particular vacation, we stopped in Atlanta, DC, Philly, Atlantic City and New York, New York, where I took the opportunity to go to the crown of the Statue of Liberty and looked out over New York Harbor. That moment felt so cool.

By that time, my oldest foster sister and my brother had been put out of the foster home on two separate occasions. My sister and my foster brother would soon follow, on two separate occasions as well, but in that order. My foster brother, Kitch (short for Kitchenhead), was still living with us during my two years of junior high. And, in total retrospect, just his mere presence in that household, during my initial years of adolescence, proved to be quite critical to me and how I understood myself as a male. Throughout my childhood, he, Harry and the rest of our big brothers in the neighborhood would rough the younger brothers up real bad if we tried to hang out with them. Of course, the decision was always ours to make, but the point of the matter was to teach us li'l boys that there's consequences to every decision you make. So, if we wanted to hang outside after the street lights came on, we could expect to get cramped up whenever we would bump heads with them at some point during the evening. It turned into a game to us. We would run at the sight of any one of them. They would eventually catch us one by one, and then together. If one of us didn't help the others who were caught, when they did catch you, the punches to the legs and arms could go on forever depending on if you helped.

During the years of 1987-1989, I participated in SUNO's Upward Bound Program for two summers. I enjoyed the program because it put good money in your pocket for doing something positive. When I was younger, I made $35 every Saturday, with a lot of my friends, working for a local cleaners. The owner employed us to drop off and pick up all his clients' clothes in his van. As I became just a bit older, I would take my $7 a week allowance and buy paint and permanent markers. I would then charge, per image, to paint Bart Simpson, Roger Rabbit and/or graffiti in Hip-Hop form on the jeans of my neighbors and friends. Unfortunately, my popularity from elementary school didn't carry over into junior high. I was outside of my own community and new to adolescence. Much of how I learned to express my interest in a female came by way of listening to mellow moods all night. There were countless R&B artists who shaped my romantic perspectives on intimacy (male and female), but my all-time favorites were Sade' and Baby-face. I felt like the sincerity in their lyrics were something that connected with the sentiments of my maturing libido. And so, I would learn to express my desires without being inconsiderate of a person's feelings.

At 13, I recall having a very honest conversation with my girlfriend at the time. I was truthful with her about my growing desires to experience sexual intercourse. She was truthful about her not being ready, and that she was being punished too often to even have the time to do so, even if she felt different. Therefore, we decided to end the relationship and remain friends because neither of us wanted nature to take its course in a way that destroys trust.

Copulation became a reality in my world during the summer of 1990. It seemed I had been on an intentional path to do so ever since this stage in my life began. Ever since junior high, me and my friends would go to the mall, to the movies, parades, Skate Country, house parties, fairs and football games just to meet females. Our hope was to charm them enough to get their phone number and make out with them somewhere secluded. Then, the phone conversations would lead to us planning to have sex.

Don't get me wrong, some would implicitly, or explicitly, send a message that the term "sex" was somehow too sensitive for us to discuss, or even think about. Rather, I should be more interested in her as a person. Overlooking the most obvious interest in her is the fact that as a person, I found her physical energy to be attractive. Therefore, if she's a "heterosexual" female, it would make sense if she felt the same way about me, and found ways to put herself in position to meet someone she's attracted to. That's just how females roll; the nature of their femininity is subtle aggression. I don't think any female would agree that she would be cool with her dude seeing her only as a sexual conquest. Us males, on the other hand, seem to think it's super macho to be viewed as such by the females.

The nature of my adolescence was like a young bull elephant by my freshman year at the selective admission high school in the seventh ward, where my foster sister had been attending since 1988. No longer was I the familiar looking, handsome li'l dude that couldn't keep up with the fashion. Now, I was the handsome young fella' that acted older than his age, hanging with my brother's best friend, and his friends, who all were junior class men. This school made school uniforms mandatory my freshman year, so all I had to do was keep a fresh pair of kicks and a fitted hat, if I didn't have a fresh cut. In junior high, my wardrobe was embarrassing. My clothes were cheap, and my shoes were plastic.

There were also a lot of students from my elementary classes accepted into this high school. No longer did schoolmates just look past me, like I didn't even exist, or look down upon me, like they wished I didn't exist. It certainly aids the esteem when you can truly feel that, more times than not, people found you to be attractive and worthwhile as a person, inside and out. I had really worked hard to show that I was much more than just a handsome face. In that pivotal moment, I was not prepared to start from scratch, in addition to the unavoidable new challenges of taming my testosterone. Subsequently, I became a bit of a slave to my physical impulses. We were going to all of the high school dances, the basketball and football games, and the school's talent show, which was such a popular event; it was officially called the "Explosion." I dared not get into that competition. It wasn't little ol' elementary school. It is was a huge school. I even shied away from trying out for my favorite sports because I didn't want to be told that I was too small in height to make the team, although I did join the baseball team.

Initially, I was keeping up with the fashion because I was getting Polo's that my foster sister didn't want, or didn't wear anymore. But, of course, that didn't last long. And mainstream socialization of the 1990's New Orleans' inner city culture seemed to demand that I find a way to keep up with my peers who had the parents to provide them with the Polo's, Bally's, leathers, suedes, gold chains, gold medallions and diamond buttercup earrings. I even had two gold teeth placed on both my upper lateral teeth in 1992. By that time, I got put out of the high school I attended during my freshman year, for failing my classes because I was so focused on getting with the females.

I was up on the phone late in the night, and cutting class to be on both lunch periods. Eventually I was put out of the foster home, the day following my 16th birthday, for being suspected of selling drugs in the neighborhood. I failed to mention that some of the biggest drug dealers in New Orleans, during the 80's and 90's grew up in Pontchartrain Park. And, if you would ask the biggest one I knew, he'd tell you that he was being supplied by the government.

April 14th, 1992, I moved in with my biological mom's eldest sister, Auntie Julia, in the eighth ward. She was named after her maternal grandmother. My mom had another older sister, and a younger brother who was due to be released from Louisiana State Prison in only a matter of months after serving

16 years. Auntie Julia stayed in a one bedroom, four-plex, upstairs, shotgun apartment with her daughter, who was only a year younger than me. My grandmother and her husband, Mrs. and Mr. Albertine and George Teapo, lived only a few blocks away, and raised my Aunt Julia's older son. My biological mom visited us regularly throughout my life. She would, mostly take us on Bourbon Street and the Riverwalk. We would catch a couple movies at the Loew's State Theater.

As a consequence of changing residences, I was not allowed to go to the high school I had attended for my sophomore year, which was Pontchartrain Park's district school. Therefore, for my junior year I ended up at Francis T. Nicholls High School (which was renamed Frederick A. Douglass about four years later). Living with my aunt my responsibilities grew quite rapidly. She gave me my own key. She gave me the responsibility of looking after her daughter, my cousin whenever we would go to the same school dances, or house parties. I also landed a part time job at a big grocery store, just across the street, making $187 a week. Therefore, I did continue to find need to supplement those wages by illegal methods. I used some of those wages to help with my summer expenses. I had taken advantage of getting more school credits during the summer in my efforts to graduate high school early. This accorded me some sense of turning my misfortunes into something positive.

After Aunt Julia gave birth to her youngest son, in April 1993, my cousin and I moved with her to her boyfriend's house in Gentilly. This home was a three-bedroom, duplex, shotgun apartment. So, I had my own room again. This same year, my younger sister gave birth to a son in February, and named him Jerome. By this time, I was heavy into sex and the night life that came along with it which was right around the time I first got involved with my son's mom. But, he wasn't born yet. No longer was I the dude that wouldn't bring girls by the house because I hated pretending that my foster mom was my grandmother who I called mom. Now I was this fella' who had a part time job, supplemented his income, was ahead in high school graduating credits, with a key to the house, responsibility over my teenage girl cousin, aggressive charm and sexual confidence.

Although I lost my part time job for not paying for items I needed out of the store. So, supplement income turned into primary income. And, that turned into a young life getting more vulnerable to the system the closer I got to 18. I was now 17.

Eventually I moved out of my Aunt Julia's home and moved into a three bedroom project apartment with a 25 year old female and her five children. This happened after my aunt found a quarter ounce of cocaine that I'd left in the bathroom.

I don't know exactly, but this couldn't be too long after I attended a sweet 16 party, where a guy was murdered and two others were shot. That happened in May. Me moving in with this 25 year old mother of five, had to be in June. Because not long after, I dropped out of summer school, but still only needed two and a half credits to graduate. Nonetheless, by the time the next school year came around, I was arrested on my biological mom's 41st birthday, while I was at the high school registering for my senior year.

My second day in Orleans Parish Prison (OPP), after I was fully processed in the system, I was placed on B-2, right side, an open flat with triple bunks. It was like one large cage with too many people living in it—Maybe 25 to 30 people! I only knew one person. We went to school together during my junior year. We never hung out or anything like that though. Of course, it felt good seeing a familiar face. However, while playing checkers with this familiar face, with my back turned away from everything, I was hit in the back of the head with a broomstick. I later found out that someone convinced my attacker that I had stolen his missing commissary.

The deputies asked me why I did it. They punched me in the stomach. As I crouched over from the blow, they rammed my head into the wall because I denied it. I needed seven stitches to close the wound where the broomstick had broken across my head. I was placed in the hole, the dungeon, lockdown, whatever they called it. I kept to myself, although I had three other people living in the cell with me. Eventually, I grew comfortable with the three people I was in the cell with.

One day I offered to wash one of their pairs of tennis shoes while I was washing my own. I mean, I didn't think anything of it. I really just needed something to do. One of my cellmates, Spider, immediately warned me about being so kind to people you don't really know. He said, "Most dudes would try and play on that." Huh? Of course, I didn't want anybody playing on me for nothing! So, I kept myself in check with being too friendly from that point on. I appreciated Spider for that. I was definitely no push-over by a long shot. I got pissed off just like everybody else, especially if you forced my hand!

One day a guy just hung up the phone on me while I was in the middle of a conversation with my girlfriend. Very loudly, he told me that it was not my turn, and that he was supposed to have used it before me. My immediate reflex was to start throwing punches and did not want to stop. Others had to pull me off of the guy. Why didn't he find a better way to handle that situation?

On hump-day, September 7th, 1994, I was pulled into Section "J" of Criminal District Court, very early in the morning to face trial. By way of the deputy sheriff, Judge Leon Canizzarro allowed me a phone call to notify my family and ask them to bring me some clothes to wear for trial. They brought me what I wore for Easter Day earlier that year: a plaid button-down short-sleeved shirt, khaki shorts, dress socks and brown loafers. I was the only person in the courtroom wearing shorts! I hadn't talked to my friends, or family about preparing for court or trial since I'd been arrested, but they were there. Actually, I never thought I would see the inside of a prison. I thought they would just call my name one day and say, "... you rollin' out!"

One Thursday evening, nine days before Christmas in 1993 the murder victim's best friend picked my picture out of a photo line-up, and stated that it was not me, because he knew me from seeing me at random teenage events. Following my release, the mother of the deceased visited the district attorney's office and New Orleans Police Department's Homicide unit, accompanied by her attorney, to express her stern disapproval towards the city for not convicting her son's murderer. Ultimately, this lead to the best friend's statement being altered to identify me as the murderer, which eventually lead to my re-arrest eight days following my 18th birthday, and me being wrongfully imprisoned.

The small possibility of me not leaving with my love ones felt really probable when I saw the cold stare of the judge's green eyes on that day. The assistant district attorneys assigned to the case were two young, white, female robots. My court-appointed lawyer was an old white man who was not prepared, not effective, not empathically competent and actually worked to get a guilty verdict. Two teenagers from the party, one of the guys who was shot and a friend of the guy who was killed, got on the witness stand and swore up and down I was the murderer. My four friends and I got on the witness stand and swore up and down that I was not guilty. Three of these guys were the ones who I was there with the entire time, and the fourth was other guy that was shot, the one I assisted after the shooting.

I'm removed from the courtroom and placed all alone in a holding cell while the jury deliberated. I was scared. The district attorney (DA) made me and my witnesses look like fools. Since we couldn't prove someone else did the shooting, I must be guilty, because the DA's witnesses seemed certain it was me, despite the facts that had shown otherwise. My mind completely shut down while I was praying to God that if they don't find me 'not guilty,' then please don't let them find me 'guilty' of second degree murder. I'll take the manslaughter conviction instead because I can't possibly handle having to serve a sentence that expects me to die in prison by the expiration of my natural life. The verdict is in, so I was awakened. Guilty as charged! My mind went blank. My heart felt doomed. Life of hard labor without the benefit of parole, probation, or suspension of sentence! I was confused. Guilty? How? Why? I'm innocent! I was on the scene after the crime, while the real perpetrator was being chased as he escaped. I had absolutely nothing to do with what happened, except trying to help a guy I knew who got shot during the fight. My 18 year old life flashed right before my eyes. "Will I ever be free again? Will I get a chance to graduate high school, go to college, get married, raise a family, to be the best uncle to my nephew and niece?" I desperately thought if we give it two, maybe three years, they'll figure this out and I'll get my life back.

When I was brought back to the tier, the guys were surprised to see me. They couldn't believe it. One guy I was friends with was also scheduled for trial soon. He always declared his innocence. I advised him to get a plea bargain. "They don't care anything about you being innocent. You're charged with the crime, you must be guilty," I told him. My friend agreed to five years of which he would only have to do two and a half. I never saw him again.

In early October that same year, I called home and heard that an ex-girlfriend of mine just gave birth to a baby boy. Her family said that he looked like me. He was born on Tuesday, October 4th. This ex-girlfriend of mine was only a few weeks into her second trimester when I'd been arrested. I was "just in" the beginning phase of a life term to which I had been sentenced on September 14, 1994. As a result, this caused Justin's birth to be much less of a joyous occasion to his mother and I, to say the least. I was an 18-year-old now plagued with the trauma of being behind bars in a distant place. I had not the slightest idea of the degree of suffering now gripping my being. She was 19-years old, newly burdened with the challenges of raising our son on her own without a clue of the stress and sacrifices that would be demanded of her heart.

Two months after I was sentenced, I was at Hunt Correctional, awaiting processing to Angola Prison. I remember my lone prayer, "Please Lord, don't put me in a position where I have to really hurt somebody trying to defend myself." I was young, small, quiet, and lost to the ways and daily operations of prison. I didn't know anybody in Angola Prison and didn't know what to expect. The only advice my aunt gave me was, " ... don't you borrow anything from anybody!"

When I first arrived at Angola, I thought I had been zapped back into the 30's with all the fields and fields of farmland and pastures, dirt roads, cows, horses, donkeys pulling wagons with an old inmate wearing a straw hat, and dingy clothes, steering its way. Mostly black men lined up two by two marching to work under the authority of rifle-toting whites on horseback. I was deeply infuriated at the conditions under which we were forced to live and work, and how it all seemed to disrupt any spirit of freedom and/or redemption. I immediately thought to myself, "This is the type of slavery I'd been taught was abolished long ago!" My initial placement was in a two-man cell with a guy who had already been incarcerated for 22 long years.

Remember, I was a rather small statured fella' at 18 years of age. Luckily, this guy's mindset was not of the normal devious nature that was typical of a lot of other older prisoners during my arrival. Which means, my cellmate didn't believe in using his experience here at Angola Prison as any kind of advantage against my naïveté. If that had been the case, I would have found myself in a dreadful predicament where I could have been easily forced to defend myself. My first week there, a guy was killed by the hands of his cellmate. To the contrary, I'd been able to feed off of my cellmate's apparent disgust with "the system."

Initially, my friends and family seemed very supportive. The matriarch of my biological family, Mrs. Albertine Teapo, orchestrated much of that support. I felt more confident in my innocence, thinking that the system is definitely going to realize this horrible mistake and release me. My cellmate had already been away from society for 22 long years. Ol' Castro was militant, wearing a red, black, and green knitted beret so proudly, covering a horrendous scar stretching from one ear to the next across the top of his head. He'd suffered the wound in a bout with security several years ago.

I was sent to the 'general population' (dormitory-style living with freedom and privileges) at the age of 19, but not without the help of an ex-girlfriend's best friend's dad. He introduced himself to me as "Writer, Nia's best friend, Keisha's daddy." Writer played for a locally known prison band named Mega Sound, a group of talented musicians who were awarded the status of trustee prisoners and played music for all of the warden's guests and even traveled to several venues outside of Angola Prison to perform. I was being housed in Oak 3 dormitory, on the West Yard/Wild Side. Writer was on the East Yard/Political Side. He said if I stayed clear of any write-ups for a period of 90 days, I could get a job other than the field work and then be moved to the East Yard.

The work in the field was much rougher now. When I was in the cellblocks, we weren't expected to do the large-scale work assignments, because the field lines were much smaller than those in general population. It went from 20-30 prisoners to almost 200 (in the fields)! I received quite a few write-ups for not working with enough speed and efficiency. I began to get the notion that the field farmers were purposely requiring the work to be done at a fast pace, knowing damn well I wasn't accustomed to doing this kind of work, just so I would get left behind. This made my attitude worse. If the pace that I was working wasn't good enough, then so be it! At least I wasn't refusing to work at all. It's not like I'm getting paid! Most of the younger prisoners stuck together, along with some of the older ones who could relate to our positions and didn't want to see any of us get stuck out and sent back to the
cells. Or maybe some of the older ones wanted to win favor. Get you to thinking he's got your best interest at heart, all the while intending to make you his possession. They call it mental gymnastics or snaking. Being coldhearted, to some, was the measure of a strong man. I wasn't so convinced. In fact, everything about that whole perception seemed weak to me. I don't like anything about the concept of taking advantage of people. It could get a lot of people hurt—Even killed. They don't even realize that's why we're here—Being taken advantage of, that is. And you find pleasure when you turn around and do it to somebody else. That's disgusting. Mentally sick!

Most of the prison population banded together by area, city, neighborhood, or what you had going for yourself. I mostly got acquainted with other guys through my love for sports, playing football, basketball, and baseball. This caused a few fights, but nothing major. I also started to teach myself to cut hair to occupy my time and to earn a few pennies to keep myself from having to ask anybody for anything. Plus, I needed some kind of outlet to attend to that artist inside of me, in addition to my ability to counsel my peers. My main problems came from security and slave labor. I always declined any help in the field; I'll gladly take the write-ups. I already had to serve the rest of my life in prison. The disciplinary board would pile me up with extra duty. That meant work on Saturdays and Sundays. Seven days a week for months at a time! Isn't that against the law? Especially since I've been wrongfully convicted!

I wanted out! I would always hear myself wondering in thought, "When are the courts going to give my freedom back, that which they have stripped from me for no reason? Am I really here in a place I believe I should never have seen for any reason?" It was indeed slavery! And racist! There were no whites even close to my age assigned to be a field hand. To tell you the truth, the jail didn't seem to have many whites in it, period, as far as I could see. The number of whites was not anywhere near the number of blacks. Whenever I did see a group of whites, they always had the better job positions and privileges.

Where were the older prisoners who could properly direct me and aid me with their wisdom? Few among many. Some of the older prisoners were even more ignorant than guys in my age bracket. Or maybe just mis-educated. My grandfather referred me to a guy that was here when he was doing time in Angola Prison. I met with the guy one day, told him who I was, and explained my situation. The guy's odor was so terrible I began to think that he hadn't showered since him and my grandpa was there together. He was no help at all.

Every single day I called my girlfriend, Shondell, collect. She, her mother, and younger sister always accepted my calls. Shondell and my cousin, Shontil, came to visit me twice a month. I got visits from my childhood friends, Rommel and Jeffery, who were with me at the party, and knew firsthand about my innocence, along with my best friend Lesley, and my Auntie Julia. My grandmother was getting old. She and my grandpa visited me with Shondell and the rest of the family, but I was troubled seeing my grandma using a walker. I was frustrated with myself for having her go through all that just to come visit me. I couldn't bear the thought of her injuring herself trying to board the prison bus. So, I had no choice but to make a request to have her name removed from my visitor's list to prevent sending her through the trouble, just for my sake.

My Auntie Julia passed away in 1996 not long after she came to visit me in prison. My foster mom passed away at some point during that time as well.

I still had a state-appointed attorney for the purpose of filing an appeal to get my freedom back. I thought that there was no need to waste money my family didn't have to hire a paid attorney. This should have been simple. Everybody knew that I was innocent. And, once the appeals court reads the record, they'll see that for themselves. In such a spirit, I started to get acquainted with two guys from out of the Desire Project. They were brothers, Sleepy and Chubby. One day we sat out on the yard, conversing while they allowed me to look through their family photos. I recognized his cousin. "She's the niece of my mother's husband," I said. I told him I went to high school with her, but I never met my mother's husband.

Chubby said, "That's our Uncle Michael." I explained that my mother was in St. Gabriel Prison and my brother seemed to also be on his way to Angola Prison. I told them, "I'm innocent." Chubby and Sleepy advised me that the appeal process is not as easy as I thought. They offered to teach me law so I could file a supplemental appeal on my own behalf. I wasn't a lawyer, so reading law cases seemed like learning a foreign language. I followed their lead. They helped me to litigate a supplemental appeal claim of "Insufficient Evidence" (Jackson vs. Virginia). I submitted this to the courts and waited. In a matter of months, I was called to pick up some legal mail from the prison package room. Appeal denied! I now had two years to file a post-conviction relief application, but only one year to preserve my right to file for relief in federal court. They taught me more about the law.

We researched, shepardizing, studied the transcript from the trial, took notes, and got advice from a couple of older guys we respected.

One weekend, in the midst of all the chaos, I was written-up for defiance and aggravated disobedience and sent to the same cellblocks that my biological brother, Harry, had arrived to, just a week prior. It all seemed so unreal, like something greater had to be in the mix. How did this happen? Harry's attitude was far worse than mine. The family was very unsupportive of him. He felt misunderstood. I tried to console him with the fact that I cared. He eventually got sent to lockdown for masturbating.

Angola Prison was a "sexual jungle." In years not long from then, it was known as the bloodiest prison in the nation. But little do people know, the emasculation of heterosexuality was to blame. In the 80's, a lot of prison same-sex rapes were being ignored. Even when I arrived at the prison, I still sensed this air about prison homosexuality being this "macho thing" as long as you didn't play the role of the female. In imitating normal gender roles in society, those who played the role of the female caused a lot of bloody fights, and killings. So intentionally pathetic, the prison administration would actually utilize this forced sexuality to keep prisoners content, and then take away the male playing the role of a female to elicit information about drug activity, who was posing some threat to security or anything else the administration was seeking to know. It's a life of "acute deprivation" and "social insignificance."

Male prisoners are forced to live a life where they are completely emasculated: no control over things that affect them; their personal desires and feelings are ignored; and deprived of "normal" avenues of gratification. No conjugal visits, or consent of any kind, from a female is permitted by prison policy. This results into an "urgent and terrible need for reinforcement of his sense of male hood and personal worth." On a quest for both, power and male hood, prisoners engage in the domination of one another. Angola Prison population consisted of men whose sexuality, sense of masculinity, and sexual frame are structured around females. Therefore, weaker prisoners are made to assume the role of the female by servicing the strong, and reinforcing the stronger's sense of male hood and personal importance. Providing the gratification of needs that would, in the normal world, be provided by females. The male prisoner who was forced to assume the role of the female becomes the property of his conqueror, a slave who must submit his entire existence to another male prisoner. In some instances, the weaker men seek out a "husband" to protect themselves from the possibility of gang rape, or forced prostitution.

Those experiences in Angola Prison, and the perverted re-creation of gender and power norms are fundamental characteristics of prisons all across the nation, including our juvenile justice institutions. So, in reality, thousands of males have absolutely no natural outlet for their sexual, emotional and psychological frustrations. This exponentially intensifies the detrimental impact of depression, suicide, inadequacy, humiliation and recidivism. Ultimately, at the cost of taxpayer dollars.

Own Thyself

When my brother was written up for masturbating, he was placed on lockdown for months. I eventually made it back to general population, by being write-up free for three months. I was placed in Pine 1 dormitory, on the West Yard/Wild Side. I was back working in the 'marching 200' field line.

I was assigned to a bunk that was next to a guy in my age range. As we got to know one another, each of us seemed to be the type of person who does all they can to provide for their own life respectfully. We instantly became friends and watched each other's backs no matter what. He was also sentenced to die in prison, which was the expected end of the majority of the guys in my age-range who were imprisoned. We were trying our best to file our own cases with the little help we got from the few who were man enough to assist without a selfish agenda. We looked out for each other and would share the little we had so that each of us at least had something decent to eat at the end of each day.

I also organized, with a group of friends who had some convict history with my friend whose bunk was next to mine. These friends lived in separate dorms on the Wild Side. Mostly all were from Downtown New Orleans. Daniel Rideau was from the Graveyard in the 17th ward, Uptown New Orleans. Me and the guys from downtown had put together a group that was supposed to represent the uncompromising principles of being a "solid" individual no matter the predicament. We functioned under the guise of being a "rap label" which only supported thought-provoking content. We called ourselves L.I.V.E. Entertainment. The acronym meant "Life Inside Violent Energy" and the opposite of it being E.V.I.L. or "Egotistical Voices Ignoring Loyalty." The "Violent Energy" is the eternal flame, and the "Life Inside" is the substance of you. The "Loyalty" is your substance. We operated similarly to a fraternity. However, I've always been a free-thinker in any of my groups of friends, but that didn't hinder the brotherhood that God had in mind for me, nor the friends I had outside of L.I.V.E.

There were also other groups of guys coming together to include areas they lived in before prison. That's what it got reduced to in all actuality. Nevertheless, Robert Jones was a standout in his own right amongst the G-Clef (Gorilla-Cheetah-Lion-Eagle-Family) arm of the L.I.V.E. movement. He excelled at the administrative tasks of the movement.

Solely due to the rearrangement of certain classes of prisoners in the Main Prison, Wild Side, I was moved to Camp C, Bear 3 dormitory. The move really set me back with filing my appeal. I was dying inside by now. Once I got settled into the new space, I filed my post-conviction relief application a day before the deadline. I submitted to the court, issues of ineffective assistance of counsel, prosecutorial misconduct, and insufficient evidence as a pro se litigant.

Meanwhile, Shondell got pregnant and was planning to get married to the father of her child. She visited me to tell me face-to-face and let me know that she wouldn't be back to visit me ever again. Of course, I gave her my blessing. The female I was involved with when I first experienced puberty, found her way back into my life. She said she had been trying to get in touch with me since my arrest. She believed in my innocence. She visited me as a friend. My little sister having gotten older began to visit me on her own as well, bringing my two nephews, Jerome, my namesake, and Ja'Mel. I earned my GED.

Suggesting to the field farmer that it would be less tenuous for the workers if we did the work in a different way, got me sent to lockdown. My suggestion incited a riot.

On top of that, my post-conviction was denied. I inadvertently mailed the application to the wrong court building. Why couldn't they just forward it to the proper court? I filed in good faith. Now the higher courts will also deny me any review because my time to file had expired since I had not "properly" filed from the beginning.

Karlas got married. I was so happy for her even though she has no more room in her life to be my friend. Then my grandmother died. I made it back to the cellblocks. My grandfather died. I get sent back to lockdown. I gather my strength and refuse to give up! Harry won his appeal. I didn't want to pressure him, but I had an idea. I started a letter-writing campaign and got my hands on a legal directory to randomly select names of Baton Rouge and New Orleans area attorneys, and other investigative agencies. I mailed them all a letter explaining my innocence.

I mailed one to my cousin, Shontil, to bring with her to a rally at the state capitol and hand out to anyone in the legal profession. I mailed one each to Rommel and Jeffery, and asked them to go to the rally as well. I mailed copies of this same letter to any and everyone I could possibly think of. I got an address to an innocence organization that had recently been formed in New Orleans, from a fellow prisoner named Chicken. I waited anxiously. I'm in contact with Tamika, the ex-girlfriend who gave birth to our son, Justin, who I had yet to meet. I was nervous, but excited too. I had gotten a few responses from Della Hayes, Lionel Berniard, Innocence Project New Orleans (IPNO) and two young New Orleans college students, Shannon and Aeryn, who were closely associated with my friend, Rommel. I responded to each one of their letters. Aeryn took full charge!

I made it back to the cellblocks. I was there for three weeks. An incident erupted at work in the field. Security wanted us to work in the rain. Policy states that once it begins to rain, the field lines are to be brought in. A couple guys refuse, Poo-man and Kevin. Security tried to approach Kevin. He struck the officer across the back with his work tool, an L-blade. Shots were fired from the gun guard. They signaled for back up. I was in close proximity to Poo-Man and Kevin. I felt that they were at too much of a disadvantage. Should I help or turn my back and walk away with everyone else? I stood there. Kevin let me off the hook by pitching me his hat and glasses while motioning me to go about my business. So many guards beat on Poo-Man and Kevin that you couldn't even see them at the bottom of the pile. A lot of broken bones, loud screams, and a lot of blood! I felt hurt. I felt dehumanized. Although I was happy not to have to go back on lockdown.

Aeryn advocated for my innocence more than anybody ever did. I felt blessed! She and Shannon sent letters to Montel Williams and Oprah Winfrey. She, Shannon, Je, and Rommel all visited me. Aeryn raised money so I could hire a private attorney. She interviewed a couple, and I instructed her not to dare give anybody any money unless they agreed to come meet with me in person. No one agreed to meet with me in person, but they all want to be hired as my attorney. No deal!

Aeryn set her sites on IPNO. She spoke with Robert Hoelsher and offered to be trained as an investigator to help them solve my case. I got subpoenaed to Jefferson Parish court to possibly testify on behalf of a guy who was once my cellmate and now was being tried for the death penalty. My testimony was not needed. But, while I was in the Jefferson Parish jail, I received a visit from my son's mother and Aeryn. After this,

Aeryn and I decide to become romantically involved. Filings remained difficult. Justice moves slowly. The pressure of being in an intimate relationship with one another mounts to high levels of frustration and impatience. There was no significant progress on my case yet. Our relationship fell apart. She got married. No more time in her life to continue helping me prove my innocence. Of course, I offered her my sincerest well wishes.

I understood. IPNO continued to keep in touch. They visited quite often: John Adcock, David Parks, Emily Maw, Richard Davis, volunteers, and interns. For some reason they refused to abandon me. They had actually become my only hope.

Harry was killed. Contact with friends and family became few and far between. I had to keep my nose clean. I had a son. I had been trying, so subtly, over the years, to persuade his mom to finally allow me to meet him. She said he was not quite ready, which really meant she was not quite ready to have to answer his questions. I didn't want to push too hard though. I was here, and she was out there. I would hate for her to just shut me out altogether. My family didn't seem to want to get involved. Yes, they knew her, but still choose to believe that her son was not mine, even though not one of them ever took the time to meet Justin. As for me, I was able to deal with the anguish of my captivity without any door of opportunity to fulfill my obligations and capacity as Justin's father. I, too, was well acquainted with the voids I had to endure while growing up without knowing my father, and words cannot explain how much I didn't want that for my own son. In that spirit, I took pride in continuing my efforts to have a presence in his life as much as I could, despite my many frustrations and the troubles I'd encountered as I struggled against the conformity of life inside Angola Prison.

Then, one day, in the fall of 2004, I was presented with the possibility of meeting my son for the very first time. The occasion was a first of its kind—an outdoor annual event catered to incarcerated fathers, providing them with quality time with their children in an attempt to reduce the rate of failure affecting children with incarcerated parents. I couldn't be sure if Justin's mother would give her consent since she'd always been against me mentioning anything about my situation to Justin. Albeit, I took a shot and submitted all the required information to the coordinator of the event with hopes that Justin's mom would grant her permission. I'd also submitted information on my two nephews and figured that if Justin wasn't allowed to come, I would just share that time with them. However, much to my surprise and delight, it was Justin who showed up and not my nephews!

It's far beyond my ability to describe the exhilaration I felt at that very moment. As I laid eyes on this handsome young fella' for the very first time, we hugged and we kissed, we conversed and laughed! He was nine years old, almost 10 and I was 28. We talked in depth about his likes and dislikes, family, my situation, and the future as if our bond as father and son had never been severed. It was such a wonderful feeling being with him, but at the same time I can starkly recall this nagging pain wrenching at my heart because I was well aware that this much awaited day would soon come to an end, and I could tell that Justin felt it too.

Well, I guess you could say that my son and I survived the torment of having to go our separate ways. In the weeks and months that followed, when I would speak with Justin and his mom over the phone, all Justin would talk about was what we would do next year when he would attend the event. Not long thereafter, a document that could prove my innocence, which was never turned over by the DA, was discovered by IPNO. I was thrilled. Before taking action, IPNO wanted to talk with the witnesses to see if they were also willing to come forth with the truth. All of a sudden, Hurricane Katrina came through the gulf and tore through New Orleans.

I, and every other prisoner from the city of New Orleans, watched in disbelief as people in our communities were being exposed of their daily grief and despair. The TV room, in the dormitory, remained eerily silent except for the occasional, "That's my auntie!" or "That's in the East," whenever one of the prisoners would recognize an area or the people being displayed on the gut-wrenching news coverage. Some guys had to pull themselves away from the TV to better deal with all the obvious questions in their minds. Who?? What? When? Where? How? Why?? Thousands upon thousands of people were being reported dead. Hospitals, nursing homes, even buried bodies being washed up out of their graves as if their death wasn't enough. The television remained on CNN for days, if not weeks. Whatever amount of days it was, felt to me like one very long day that just didn't want to end. A few guys stayed put in the TV room with their attention sternly affixed to the developing news without ever even considering one wink of sleep. The dorm held 64 prisoners with only one TV. Eventually, other prisoners from other areas around the state or elsewhere wished to be watching the regular programs again. This caused offense to quite a few prisoners from New Orleans and resulted in arguments that quickly escalated into fights. Quite naturally, there was a great sense of desperation amongst all of us who had family and friends living in those affected areas, and we were so very eager to hear any news that would indicate that our people were alive!

Initially, the Angola administration had no answers to bring calm to the growing frustrations. The phone lines in the city were down, and New Orleans area post offices were inoperative. Some of the more considerate prisoners who had family and friends, in unaffected areas that they could call collect, offered to try and contact some of the family and friends of the prisoners from the city. These very kind efforts urged the Angola administration to set up "link lines" in each security office on every unit for us to use to try and contact our loved ones free of charge. Within days, Angola also became a shelter for New Orleans area parish prisoners with funds allocated by FEMA and other recovery organizations. At the time, I was in steady contact with a female friend named Shanika, who lived in LaPlace, an area not at all affected by Katrina. Therefore, after not being able to contact any of my family members directly, I would utilize the "link lines" to call her and get updated concerning my sister and nephews, my son, my niece, my mom, my cousins, my aunt, any IPNO office members, and Mrs. McWilliams, a lady who I very dearly consider as family because she had kept in contact with me since I was placed in Angola Prison. She was the foster mother of my deceased brother and also continued to support his daughter, my only niece.

The very first person I remember hearing from after Katrina was Mrs. McWilliams. She contacted me September 3rd, 2005, letting me know that she was okay, after deciding to leave her home in New Orleans East at 3:30 AM Sunday, to evacuate to her daughter's home in Gonzales. She also informed me that her other family made it out okay, but she wasn't so sure about my niece, and her family, because she hadn't heard from them. In her letter, she also conveyed some of the same images from the CNN news reports and expressed her suspicions about the breeches to the levees and the resentment she felt towards Washington for being so slow with sending help to the city. So, we continued to correspond through letters and would update one another on any and all information we could find on any of the others.

The very next person to contact me was my mother. For the most part, one would think that this shouldn't be strange. However, before Katrina, I hadn't heard from my mom since 1997! Back then, she was serving time in St. Gabriel Prison, and the woman's prison would afford them a trip to Angola Prison twice a year to visit any immediate relatives. We visited once, and she was released that same year. This time I received correspondence from her expressing motherly sentiments, while also informing me that she was in the parish jail when the hurricane hit, and that they were evacuated to Angola Prison. She also made note to ask if I had any information on any of our family. Excited to be contacted by my mother, despite the lapse of time, I immediately brought her letter to the attention of the security supervisor over the camp and asked that he would allow me to be transported to Camp F, where my mother was being sheltered, so that I could visit with her. My request was granted, and I, along with a few others who had immediate relatives being sheltered at Camp F, were transported there almost twice a month. I was also allowed to provide her with any necessities that she needed. Shanika was even kind enough to mail money to her account so that she could afford to purchase the feminine products that I couldn't possibly provide. We really made the most of these visits in our reconciliation as mother and son, until Angola Prison transferred her to a Simmsport area jail, where she was soon released.

The very first time I received any signs of life concerning my sister and her sons was through a November 22, 2005 letter from Shanika, telling me that she'd received information online that my sister was located in Virginia. She called the number and left a message. On December 4, 2005, I received a letter from Shanika telling me that she had finally talked to my sister on her birthday, November 30th. She said that my sister expressed disbelief that Shanika had actually tried to track her down and was surprised to hear her voice on her voicemail. She said that my sister was eager to know how I was doing and even told Shanika that she couldn't think of where in the world our mother could be. So Shanika informed her that our mother was doing fine and explained that whole situation to her. Also in Shanika's letter, she told me how my sister expressed how lonely and depressed she had gotten until speaking to Shanika, and that surely now she and my nephews were okay. I then urgently called Shanika on the "link line" and got my sister's number so that I could speak with her myself. The next day, I was finally able to hear my sister's voice and talk with my nephews. They told me that they rode the storm out at home, and there was not significant damage to their home, but they were made to evacuate under the state-of-emergency and ended up on the Claiborne Bridge, before being taken to Virginia. We kept updated with one another and later gathered information on my cousins and aunt who evacuated to our cousin's home in St. Louis. In September 2007, Shanika quite pleasantly surprised me with a visit, accompanied by my sister and nephews. That was the first time I saw them after Katrina. Through a letter dated June 18, 2006, Mrs. McWilliams provided me with my niece's address, and, of course, I took the privilege of writing to her, which began our very first moments of getting to know one another.

I had gotten IPNO's contact information in September 2005, from another client of theirs, whose case was being represented by them in court at that time. Of course, the proceedings were momentarily stalled due to the catastrophe left by Hurricane Katrina in all matters of life and liberty in New Orleans. However, I wrote to them at a temporary address in Jackson, MS. Everyone was devastated, but doing fine. Most of the staff were scattered about in different locations across the country, such as LA, Houston, Milwaukee, and Oregon. They extended their thoughts and prayers to me and my family, assuring me that they would continue to keep in touch and update me on any progress gathering resources and figuring out where to go from there. The office had survived the flood waters, so everyone's files were still intact. Indeed, I was very much relieved to know that no one at IPNO suffered any major loss. I had really developed a genuine relationship with them over the years. However, the situation seemed so much more daunting now, as I imagined them being even more under-staffed and under-funded due to Katrina's aftermath. Not to mention, court buildings, records offices, and evidence rooms being in ruin. In addition to the 80 plus individuals listed in the police reports who so desperately needed to be interviewed, now they were probably displaced who knows where, if they were still alive. Nevertheless, IPNO's investigation into my case picked up again in October 2006. Ebony joined IPNO and regained some momentum in my case. She inspires me with news of Resurrection After Exoneration (RAE) Foundation being legally established which will serve as transitional housing and additional services for those returning from prison. She encouraged me to get a degree in graphic arts.

In the process, I got sent to lockdown for being caught with a cellular phone. Collect calls from Angola are extremely expensive and I did not want to be a financial burden on my family and friends.

Still to this day, I'm not sure who my father is. My mother has always told me that a guy named Anderson Ross was my father. However, my last name indicates that the guy my mother is still legally married to, but long ago separated from, may very well be my father instead. Some might ask, how I have the nerve to question my mother's words on such a matter. Well, I do have my reasons, some of which I'll try my best to explain. However, for the most part, now being a grown man, I can understand that there's so much more that my mom can't quite bear to share with me concerning her physically, mentally, and emotionally turbulent times of childhood, marriage, and giving birth. My mom grew up without receiving any formal education whatsoever, was married at the age of sixteen, and her first child was stillborn, before later giving birth to my brother, Harry, at the age of twenty-one, me at the age of twenty-three, and my sister, whom she named after herself, at the age of twenty-five. All this, only to later give us all over to foster care, when we were toddlers, so that her own inadequacies wouldn't impede upon her hopes of us being properly raised and educated.

My mother's life is a puzzling story to say the least. I'm not certain exactly why she never received a school education, or why she was married so young, exactly when she separated from her husband, or when she began her relationship with Anderson Ross. When I was seventeen I had the chance to meet Anderson Ross. Back then, my mother was incarcerated for allegedly killing an abusive boyfriend, and Anderson was just being released from Angola Prison for an armed robbery sentence he had been serving all of my life. Somehow, he contacted my brother after his release, and my brother helped him to get in touch with me. At the time, I was staying with my mom's eldest sister and Anderson was living with his wife in New Orleans East. He reached me by phone to ask if he could come over and pick me up. I didn't have a problem with that, so I put him on hold to first get consent from my aunt. To my surprise, she expressed a rather strong disapproval due to what she told me was a very troublesome relationship that he had with my mom before his incarceration. However, my aunt was still considerate enough to suggest that if I indeed had my own desire to meet him, I could just tell him that I would be waiting at a nearby gas station. I then returned to the phone to relay these stipulations to

Anderson. He happily agreed, and assured me that he was on his way as soon as we ended the call.

Of course, my mind wondered about this mysterious man that my mom had always acknowledged as my father. Albeit, my heart was quite the contrary, due to all the years I had lived without both my parents' presence up to that particular point. My sentiment concerning the whole situation was that I didn't expect anything at all. In my mind, I began to think that this was more about him getting the chance to meet me instead of me having the chance to meet him. As far as I was concerned, the times I needed him most had passed. I wouldn't say I was bitter towards him in any way for being absent, because I know all too well the misfortunes of the poor and the realities that result. Therefore, I gave him and my mother the benefit of the doubt that those hardships were just as much to blame for me never having their presence to depend on. Some might say this is nothing but a child being in denial, and just simply making excuses to better cope with the pain. However, others might say this is a child, mature beyond his years, to be so considerate of what the circumstances may be that contributed to this loss.

Anderson pulled into the gas station, accompanied by my brother, in a relatively brand new red Ford Probe. We greeted sort of placidly as I got in the back seat. He then drove to a check cashing place on Canal Street so my brother could cash the check he had received from his job. We just rode around the city a bit, as I mostly kept silent except to answer questions he would ask about me and my sister, who had just given birth to her very first child. The majority of the time, I just listened to how excited my brother seemed to be, while conversing with him, as he drove us to his wife's residence in the East.

Anderson and his wife were married while he was in prison. We were all introduced, and she introduced us to her son who was fathered by another man. Her son was between me and my brother's ages and had his own used car. So us three decided to hop in his ride and stop by my brother's girlfriend for most of the day. When Anderson finally brought me back to the gas station later on that night, he first stopped by his mom's apartment, in an apartment complex directly across the street from the gas station. He introduced me and my brother to her, as she hugged and kissed us both with grandmotherly affection. But, to tell you the God-honest truth, I didn't quite feel any type of innate connection to this guy, Anderson.

From that day on, I only saw him on one other occasion, before I was arrested. And later, while I was in Angola Prison, my brother, Harry, revealed to me that when Anderson got news of my arrest, he made a very sarcastic comment to my brother, saying, "Shit, he could've let me get that reward money for his arrest." Now I definitely had something to feel bitter towards him about! I certainly couldn't understand why a father would make such a comment about his very own son's arrest. Especially, due to the fact that I am actually innocent of the crime I was arrested for. Unfortunately, not long thereafter, Anderson was murdered. Angola Prison didn't allow me to attend his funeral, but I was mailed a copy of his obituary, which listed me, my brother, and my sister as his children, among the other children he had.

I would later meet the mom, father, and older sisters, who were my mom's sister-in-law, brother-in-law, and nieces, during visitation. They were visiting brothers from their family. I was sharing a visit from my own sister, and they all expressed this very same sentiment about my resemblance to my mom's husband. No, nothing further ever came about after making these connections. From what I did gather, my mother's husband was a terribly ill man, suffering from alcohol-related health issues. Of course, I expressed my sincere concerns, although I was indeed careful not to push too hard and only end up being disappointed again by any sense of disinterest or whatever on his part.

In 2008, there was this young, Connecticut-born, former Tulane law school intern, who was hired as IPNO's staff attorney, and assigned to resuscitate my case. After a couple of years of her, Kristin's, persistent, but failed, attempts to interview key witnesses, Mosi was then called to the rescue. He was a local guy who grew up in the upper ninth ward. As he investigated, he found out that he used to be a child who attended the day care that belonged to the mother of the victim who had been fatally shot. So, he knew her personally. He also had associations with many of the mutual acquaintances of the key witnesses. During a interview that was arranged by a mutual friend, the DA's main witness admitted that he had been pressured by the detectives to lie and identify me as the shooter. I was informed of this turn of events via visitation, the day after I completed a 40-day spiritual fast, in which I had prayed for such a thing to happen. I had also been journaling and reading a chapter of Rick Warren's "Purpose Driven Life" each day.

When I made it back to the cellblocks, the Red River flooded. Angola Prison had to evacuate prisoners from the cellblocks to Avoyelles Correctional in Cottonport, LA. Around that time, IPNO finally felt that we had enough legal ground to file the new evidence proving my innocence into court. Soon after we were returned to Angola Prison.

Mosi provided me with a copy of a book written by teachers and students. It is entitled, "The Long Ride." It taught me about events and people in my city's history that I never knew. I was so moved by their writing, I wrote something to them in response. By that time, I had kept my nose clean enough to make it back to dormitory status. I then immediately got the job of being the prison cellblock barber through my boy, and fellow inmate, Donald DeGruy. He gave me a recommendation to the ranking officer of the prison who assigns those positions. My job was to regularly shave and cut all the guys' hair in the cellblocks from seven in the morning 'til five in the evening, Monday thru Saturday, and sometimes on Sunday. I would also cut hair on my own time to provide for my daily necessities. Yes, I aspired to continue being a barber even after my exoneration. For the most part, immediately following my release, I expected that this skill would allow me to earn an honest living, and eventually afford me with financial security once I was licensed to do so. Therefore, I viewed my prison job fulfillment as preparation for what was ahead once I regained my freedom. I even mapped it all out on paper.

By this time, a hearing was granted, on the case, by the court on November 14, 2011. Through Mosi, I was given the opportunity to connect with a lot of really wonderful people. Most were students. I was corresponding with almost 30 individual students, helping them along in their Critical Writing syllabus, and their life outside of the classroom. They planned to attend my hearing, my very first time back in court with a new judge—Judge Darryl Derbigny presiding.

It had been 18 years, and I was 18 years old back then. The hearing would be strictly concerning when the new evidence was discovered, and if it had been brought into court in a timely manner. My attorneys, Emily and Kristin, thought it would be good if I would testify to give the judge a chance to view my character while both sides were questioning me. I thought it was a good idea.

I was so nervous. I tried my best to calm myself, but the courtroom was freezing. I was chained up like a monster and wasn't permitted to wear any undergarments under the short-sleeved, orange prison suit. I started shaking so much that I began to hear the chains that I was wearing beginning to rattle. I looked back into the audience and smiled at my family. I really needed their strength. Between my nervousness and the temperature, I couldn't seem to get myself settled. I started doubting myself, thinking maybe I shouldn't take the witness stand. I didn't want to mess everything up and look like a fool, but I did need to speak. I had been waiting for this opportunity for far too long. But, just as I began to entertain my doubtfulness, I heard a crowd of people arrive in the audience section of the courtroom. They sounded like an army—Better yet, a community! It was some of the students and educators who wrote The Long Ride and many more students from two different high schools, wearing their school uniforms. A deep-hearted smile appeared on my face. Their presence was nothing less than a gift from God. I felt an enormous sense of empowerment. They didn't let me down, so I knew I wouldn't let them down.

At that first court appearance, I also received quite a few letters from the students. I very eagerly read them during the two hour drive back to

Angola Prison. No doubt, I appreciated them all. However, two of these letters have remained in my mind and heart to this very day.

December 1, 2011 was the continuance to this post matter procedure. Just as the transportation unit I was riding in approached the intersection of Tulane Avenue and South Broad Street and slowly made a right hand turn at the traffic light, I noticed two teenage students, female and male, jogging across the intersection together, making sure to keep up with each other, and rather hurriedly walking across the courthouse lawn and hastening up the concrete steps into the courthouse. I thought this to be sort of peculiar, because they were wearing the exact same type of school uniforms that were worn by one group of public school students who had attended my first court appearance, not even a month ago. This caused me to ask myself if they could very well be here in my interest once again? Oh, yes, it certainly mattered because I had experienced a very unforgettable moment of being much more strengthened by the empowering presence of those high school teenagers who showed such great interest in my life and cared so deeply about seeing me exonerated. Their support moved me in a way that a child is expecting of their parents to do what is necessary, to overcome troubles and provide them with their example of encouragement, so they would know how to do the same as they encounter their own difficulties. Every last one of these children had to be the same age as my own child, or very close to it.

Friday morning, January 17, 2014 the honorable Judge Darryl Derbigny ruled according to the law. He overturned my conviction and set the matter for a new trial. This decision was based on very strong evidence that police convinced and coerced two teenagers into falsely identifying me, along with evidence that the then prosecutor hid the call log record that would have proven I couldn't have managed to "escape the scene while being chased, hop a fence, stash a gun and return to the scene before the police arrived, without being noticed." The assistant district attorney voiced his intent to file a writ of appeal, arguing to the Court of Appeals and the Louisiana Supreme Court that Judge Derbigny's ruling should be overruled and reversed. My attorney then requested a bond hearing by submitting a motion for bond reduction, while the ADA pursued the prosecutor's appeal for purposes of the record: at same legal jargon that sounds like a fucking foreign language concerning a person's liberty. Orleans Parish DA's Office should have been recused since filing the newly discovered evidence in the first place, due to the Orleans Parish District Attorney being no other than the person who presided as judge during my trial in 1994.

All the while, I was still caught up in what had just happened. "Judge Derbigny really did grant me the justice I'd been praying for since that day the New Orleans Police Department (NOPD) wrongfully locked my wrists in handcuffs back when I was 17," I said to myself as that moment just froze in time. I couldn't believe it! Then my internal excitement was snapped back into the current adversarial proceedings, and my soul wondered how long it would be before I could experience the moment of my actual release from prison: Angola State Plantation and this hell-chamber they call Orleans Parish jail? Many people were in my corner. We were prepared to present all those who would comprise of my immediate environment. This included the person I would be staying with in Pontchartrain Park, along with the person whom I would work for and receive on-the-job training as a barber apprentice until I obtained my license. Exactly what I had been doing, for the most part, to provide for myself in Angola prison for the last 20 years. We didn't know if we would be making a property bond with one of my cousin's properties, or if we would be trying to raise the money to place a cash surety bond. However, when it was all said and done, we were able to post bond by the latter means and get me the hell out of there!!!

Judge Derbigny ordered: "As to Jerome Morgan, bond in this matter is set in the amount of $25,000, cash, property, or commercial surety. Special conditions will require home incarceration. You will be subject to a curfew of your activities, as well as all the appropriate restrictions as determined by the electronic monitoring authorities. I'll also require that you drug-test once a week, sir, during the course of bond." However, this order was left up to interpretation.

I ended up seeing my first air of the outside world at six p.m. on the very next day, February 4, 2014. Inside myself, I was a nervous wreck from the time the judge granted the bond reduction that prior morning until I was finally called to be released.

"Jerome Morgan, pack ya shit...you rollin' out," said the young deputy sheriff early that February morning. I didn't dare act surprised, but my smiling soul was no less delighted! I was really finally getting out of prison. All the guys gave me their farewells like captives hoping to one day be rescued and led into redemption by the community. I also thought of the guys back in Angola wishing me well, when I left there for good at five a.m. on the day the conviction was later thrown out, January 17th. The young OPP deputy, who became more familiar with my case since I was in OPP quite often within those 27 months, also gave his farewell. In total, I had traveled back and forth there to attend the two rounds of court hearings ten times between November 11, 2011 and February 4, 2014, a span of 823 days.

I appeared in court a total of seven times from the time I was arrested until I was given a mandatory life sentence, a total of 131 days. I guess it's fair to say that it's far easier to lose your freedom than it is to regain your freedom.

The deputy processing me out of the booking station gave the clothes that I initially wore to me. I was kept in a large stinky holding cell all that morning. Next I was called out into a back area where there were three bathroom stalls to change out of the prison jumpsuit, and into your own clothes that you wore when you were arrested. There were two other guys processing out as well that morning, but by evening they were gone. Of course the deputy behind the thick glass window who retrieved prisoner's personal clothes could not find any clothes belonging to me. Then he asked, "What size do you wear?" I wasn't really sure because the Angola sizes I'd been wearing for 20 years are so irregular. Nonetheless, he was able to find me a gray oversized undershirt, and a pair of gray cargo trousers that weren't pants, but too long to be considered as a pair of shorts. That very first air of the outside world, minus the handcuffs and shackles, took place as I was processed out through the Electronic Monitoring Program's (EMP) office on Dupre Street. My attorneys, much of the office staff, and several of my family and friends, were all there to greet me. Each of us were taking in the moment, hugging, kissing, and emoting tears of joy before carrying the moment over to my childhood friend's house, which would be my home during this crucial period of re-entry/reintegration/transition/restoration/healing/adaptation/re-enfranchisement. Instead of the metal handcuffs and shackles, I wore a waterproof electric monitoring ankle bracelet, or electronic shackle for short. The only things I carried with me were an electric cord to charge the electronic shackle for two uninterrupted hours each day, my most recent casework, a couple personal mail items I received recently, and a few photos that I had all in a plastic bag. Everything else, which was all a bunch of journals, writings, Xerox-copied books, the rest of my personal photos, and personal letters from loved-ones dating back to 1996, I left with a friend in Angola Prison until further notice. Whatever else I had I gave away.

After many hugs and kisses, I changed into a blue and white striped polo shirt, blue Levi's jeans, and Van's sneakers that my loved ones had brought for me to change into. I changed into boxers, socks and everything right there on Dupre Street, in the back of one of the attorney's car. Then I threw the other clothes into the garbage. After taking photos, talking, and laughing, I loaded into my cousin's very nice, and roomy, black Cadillac truck for the ride home. Home! Wow! Riding home that night was as smooth as I had always remembered. No ordinary prisoner was permitted too many opportunities to be out at night, as you would suppose. So not to be imprisoned under the night sky was definitely precious to me. We first stopped at a gas station. Yeah, I knew where I was of course, but the feeling was so damn long overdue! Plus, a lot didn't look as familiar as I remembered, like the construction of a Wal-Mart taking up the Gentilly Woods Mall space, and these Arab-owned stores on all three corners from the bank.

There were about three carloads of us, so when we stopped at the gas station one of my other childhood friends went to get the Popeye's' chicken I asked for. Popeye's, McDonald's, Rally's, Burger King, the Daiquiri Shop—all those places had been there for 21-22 years, at least. Now they have gas stations, a real hoodie strip mall, with a Brother's, Beauty Mart, and a Washateria in it. There's an Athletes Foot, Waffle House, Taco Bell, Wendy's, Winn Dixie, Soul Train Fashion, Citi Trends, and a whole bunch of other stores that were not present in 1993. I knew that out of all the delicious food in the world there is to eat, wanting New Orleans famous fried chicken might sound 'ignorant' to some conscious folks, but if you ate prison food for years and years, you'd be craving New Orleans famous fried chicken too—That's if you are used to deliciously fried you'd eaten from birth. They have some swamp folk in Angola Prison that can eat raw snake. Trust and believe.

We got the chicken, and the liquor (because you know we didn't stop at the gas station for gas), and proceeded to the house. My friends have always been there when I really needed them. One is married with a daughter and two sons. The other is married, but currently separated, with an eight year old daughter. Both are loving fathers. Both are true friends. Both are my brothers and have suffered along with me through this every step of the way. Without their love, true friendship, and brotherhood, I would not have been able to survive a quarter of the weight of this ordeal.

So, we were all mobbed up at the place where I stay, because one of the restrictions I received at the EMP office was an eight p.m. curfew. The judge ordered that I should not work, nor enroll in any kind of schooling. I was to pay $10 and submit drug samples once per week. Don't forget to include the $2350 I owed in bond payments of which I paid $440 per month, not counting interest. I was in the red all the way around the board: Financially, technologically, socially amongst friends and family and with overall knowledge of how society functions in parts and as a whole. At 37 years of age, I had never lived a life as an adult outside of being a prisoner! 19, 20, 21, 22, 23, 24, 25, 26, 27, 28, 29, 30, 31, 32, 33, 34, 35, 36, and 37 were all years I developed under very detrimental circumstances. In prison, believing I could acquire $20,000 from family, friends, and the community to start out with, I drafted a four-part two year transition plan that outlined the income I'd be able to earn cutting hair getting paid at least $11 an hour and 40 hours a week. Based on that I outlined the expenses I would be able to afford i.e., transportation, rent, utilities, groceries, clothing, furniture, etc., and how much I could commit to save each month, gaining more stability and self-sufficiency, six months at a time. And, by the two-year mark of being free, I would be ready to apply for a small business loan to start my own barbershop.

Unfortunately, my bond restrictions left that plan null and void. I was made to notify my monitoring office every time I wanted to leave the house. I was only allowed to visit my mom in Slidell, attend church, court dates, and meetings with the attorneys. I was not allowed to attend any social gatherings whatsoever: All-Star game, Congo Square Festival, IPNO Gala, Mardi Gras Ball—None of that!

Many people came to the house to celebrate. People I hadn't seen in ages—Some of whom I could never forget, others of whom I vaguely remembered or couldn't quite recollect and even a few of whom I had just met. In the next four or five days, more loved ones came, even those from out-of-state. I literally didn't sleep a wink for four days straight! We had
a celebration on consecutive nights for the first few days. It was such a thrill! I was still going through moments of thinking I'm only dreaming and had a deep appreciation for life, sharing it all with these amazing human beings. Nevertheless, I still was not "free."

That late afternoon my attorneys had press interviews set up for me, with WWL Channel 4 New Orleans ("After 20 years, wrongfully convicted man sees freedom"), NOLA.com ("Man convicted of 1993 Sweet 16 birthday shooting granted new trial; DA vows to appeal"), The

New Orleans Advocate ("Taste of freedom after 20 years"), The Advocate ("New Orleans prisoner granted new trial in 1993 murder"), and the Times-Picayune ("After 20 years, a taste of life beyond jail") all at once. But before giving the interviews, in the conference room of our attorney's office, I had Parkway 'po-boys' for lunch with all the staff from my attorney's office, and three of my exonerated brothers of years past.

While doing the interview, I couldn't help but think of how much people need to know that there's a plantation going on in prison, and a prison going on inside the minds of our society. I thought about how much I needed to catch up with my life, catch up with my family, my mom, my son, my sister, nephews, nieces, cousins, aunts, and uncles. I thought about bridging the gap between the actions that reach back for other wrongfully convicted persons (and those convicted and released, ready to move onward and upward), and the bridges that reach out to these children who've probably seen some awful shit, had absolutely no childhood, and were struggling through far more physiological abuse than the average adult mind can tolerate.

A couple days after my release, I was able to visit my mom. My sister accompanied me. Oh, how joyous that moment was for us! I was even "allowed" to stay some time after the eight p.m. curfew. However, I had to prepare my mind to convince my heart to leave. We rolled back to "my house" with smiles and more to celebrate. In the next couple weeks, I completed the Odyssey House Louisiana, Job Readiness & Sustainability Training—Something that taught me how to send e-mails, (parkroots@prkrootsproductions.com), apply for FAFSA, WIA grants, Job One/LA Works, DCFS/SNAP benefits. I learned how to do my resume, cover letter, and complete job applications. Unfortunately, all my applications ended up repeatedly being rejected for no given reason. The student assistance applications, and job opportunities were abandoned once the judge denied in part the defense motion to modify conditions of bail. The part he did modify was drug testing from once a week to once a month. I still had no chance to earn a living or furthering my education.

Within a month's time, I hit the road with the investigator. During the course of his assignment on my case, from 2010 until now, he had became to be like the little brother I never had, and I the big brother he'd never had. For those who perceive the older the generation to be the one with the ability to share and pass on knowledge to the next generation, one might agree that I may be viewed as the younger brother and he the older in many aspects of our exchange of knowledge, but by any measure, brothers indeed! He was divorced and had an eight year old daughter. He's a great father with a super spirit!

Since he was no longer working for IPNO, and held the position of case manager for the Odyssey House's Re-Entry for the Ex-Offender (RExO) Program, he signed me up, and then was responsible to assist in my re-entry process.

This seemingly coincidental circumstance was right on time. I'm telling you my initial days, if not weeks, were all just one recurring excitement. Sometimes I feel the same excitement still recurring to this very day.

With help from many supporters, I was able to get my birth certificate, social security card, state ID, clippers, liners, other barber equipment, iPhone 4, gmail account, and open a Chase liquid debit account all within the first week. You should have seen me trying to get these things for the very first time at 37, having to explain to, and sometimes argue with, the workers as to why I didn't have some of these ordinary proofs of identity. All I had was newspaper articles about my release, from the copies my friend was buying by the stacks, so we could have them on hand as much as we needed, in order to confirm my predicament to those that had to know.

My first couple days out, I went to visit McMain's and McDonogh's 35's SAC AP English classes. These were the same classes that wrote to me while in Angola, attended my very first day back in court November 2011, and wrote letters to the judge. Of course, these were not the same students. Those students, whom I corresponded with when I was imprisoned, were now in college. Two of these students are like my very own children, who went on to Bard College in Upstate New York. I'm still in contact with them both. I've attended the current SAC classes with the both of them when they come home. Being able to attend the SAC classes in person was so powerful, healing, encouraging, and up lifting. That single day turned into many.

Through the RExO Program, I was able to go to the Odyssey House Clinic on North Tonti Street where I received a clean bill of health, including negative STD/HIV results. I also started my deep gum cleaning at Daughters Of Charity dental clinic, received the Medicaid card I applied for, and attended sessions with a licensed social worker (LCSW) and opened Chase checking and savings accounts. The accounts were needed because there were two sites set up allowing folks to donate money and order personal items for me including clothes, books, or anything, straight from Amazon.com.

The sites were GiveForward ($4,425 from 37 gifts) set up by IPNO, and YouCaring ($2,154) set up by a close member of my support team outside of IPNO. All of this money went to bills I had already accrued, like the $2,350 I owed for the remainder of the bond, and the $70 and accruing debt I owed for drug testing. Over $1500 of that money went towards rent and utilities, almost $400 to obtain my driver's license, and the rest to a order various miscellaneous purchases. For a good couple of weeks, I received gifts from generous, compassionate, affiliates of IPNO, those I knew, and people from all over the country. It actually felt like Christmas in February with all the UPS/FEDEX packages that were arriving in bunches every day.

Fast forward to Friday, September 19, 2014: I received a text at 4:38 p.m., from my monitoring officer, stating that as of Sept. 21st she would no longer be my monitoring officer. She was promoted to another division of the Deputy Sheriff's Office, and my case would be assigned to another deputy. Of course, I gave her my congrats, but I hated to lose her as my monitoring officer because she and I had developed such a healthy, understanding, and respectful rapport with one another. The transition from one deputy to another was going smoothly, until the new monitoring officer texted me, "Go inside," at 11:49 a.m., on Tuesday, October 14th. I immediately called him and asked, "Why?" He said that there was no indication in my folder that the judge ordered me a curfew; therefore, I would need to abide by the rules of 24/7 home incarceration until the judge's stipulations were clarified. Quite naturally, this made me livid because how could I cut hair independently, take care of my daily necessities, and visit SAC classes if I was not allowed outta the house? However, I kept my composure and complied with the deputy's instructions. First, I went to my attorney's office to check for any record of the judge's stipulations. No such record was found! There was actually no record of my release, or the judge's stipulations, so we would have to request a transcribed copy of the judge's order from the judge's clerk. This request could take weeks, so I drove to the EMP office to notify the deputy. At the end of the day, the supervisor would agree to monitor my ankle bracelet until the transcribed copy of the judge's stipulations were furnished to my attorney.

On Tuesday evening, November 4th, I received a text from my attorney, "I've got the transcript of the ruling at the bond hearing. It says home incarceration subject to a curfew of your activities. It doesn't say 24/7, but it doesn't specify an exact curfew either." The next day, I swung by the IPNO office to retrieve this transcript to bring to the EMP supervisor. I really believed that the transcript fully clarified that the judge intended for the EMP office to use its discretion concerning my restrictions.

"As to Jerome Morgan...special conditions will require home incarceration. You will be subject to a curfew of your activities, as well as all the appropriate restrictions as determined by the electronic monitoring authorities." I was really excited as I drove to show this to the monitoring office. However, to my surprise, the EMP supervisor felt the need to contact the judge directly to confirm the legitimacy of this document. He said that he would notify me after he spoke to the judge.

The evening of the very next day, I received a text message from the EMP supervisor, notifying me that I should return home, and to report to court with my attorney at nine a.m. the following morning. Accompanied by my attorney, and a female friend, I was there at nine a.m. sharp. Once there was a break in the court docket, the judge side-barred with my attorney. Judging by the facial expressions and body language from both my attorney and the judge, I could tell that things were not looking good. Now the judge wanted my attorney to get a written request whenever I needed to leave the house.

After that, I was only allowed to leave the house for dental and therapist appointments. The judge did approve a 9 p.m. curfew from December 21st through December 26th, and from noon to six p.m. to visit my mom on January 17th. In addition, he denied my request to spend Thanksgiving in Houston with my family, as well as to attend the American Education Research Association's December workshop that I was invited to in Chicago (all expenses paid). This workshop was to highlight how the students got involved and made a positive impact on the results of my case, and the dynamics of that reciprocation. It's been quite a task to remain calm about this illogical/insult-to-injury that my loved ones and I had to continue to endure, while the prosecution dragged this matter on so unnecessarily and cold-heartedly. Shouldn't I be content with not being in OPP or Angola any longer? I'd been patient for all this time, what's a few more months? Would any human being be satisfied with the situation up to this point if it were them, or someone they knew?

Well, as of this writing, I'm personally at the compensation/civil rights suit phase. Yes, I say "phase" because this procedure happens to be everybody's cry. So, much is going to waste because so many people are trying to rip people off, to only get ripped off themselves. Then, we support "get tough on blacks because we don't want them with their own governance" type of lifestyle. It should make you think, "Why do we, the world, fear even the idea of blacks having their own, equal to any other pigment, nation of human beings?" Do we not thrive exponentially as a group, if we respect each other? There's so many examples of truth, amongst just our history here, as we continue to fight our way out of the "psychological slave machine" that the "real criminal" has raped our spirits with, that we remain "real gentlemen" because we have no hate in our heart no matter the weapon you try to use against us.

Notice that God made man: male and female. So a "gentlemen" is not gender specific, although we are very specific in God's natural order of procreation as it becomes in the likeness of the Creator of Nature that you hold your faith to. The race of Blacks that we have demoralized, and the social systemic instruments used to execute this demon they call supremacy, has given the "real gentlemen" every reason to be nothing but a "real criminal." But, when I ask black youngsters what they want to be, they tell me they want to be "real gentlemen" who have their own businesses and take care of their family, before they ever say they want to be a "real criminal" and go to jail for the rest of their lives, or be killed for something that's not worth it in the end.

Nonetheless, the "real criminals" behind mainstream socialization are teaching our children how to be "stupid cattle" carrying the image of the "real criminal." If I could ask for anything that would give me justice in my case, it would be that everyone use my triumphs in all my experiences, as examples of people coming to together utilizing their "free-dem" in a way to change the injustices of their surroundings, and live by the same faith so we can have a "just" governance. Let's seal the cracks ourselves.

We are freed men.

We are no longer enslaved by the ills of our society.

We believe in the sacristy of truth.

We pledge our lives to do what is right.

We stand tall and rise above it all.

We accept our responsibility.

Like a man.

Divided we are conquered, but together we stand.

Like a man.

Like a man.

Like a man.

—Jerome Morgan

Your Free Gift

To show our appreciation we've put together a free gift for you.

It is a compilation of sayings we wrote while in prison and since our releases. We hope that among these words you will find comfort, inspiration and the empowerment you seek.

http://unbreakableresolvebook.com/freegift

Just visit the link above to download it now.

Thanks!

Robert Jones, Daniel Rideau, Jerome Morgan

Author Bios

Robert Jones is a 44-year old African American true gentleman and native of New Orleans, Louisiana. He grew up poor and lived in distressed neighborhoods as a youth. Robert is the eldest of five other siblings; four living and one deceased. He also suffered the loss of his father when he was only seven years old. As a result, he was raised by his single-mother. The hardships of poverty and typical life experiences ultimately led him to dropping out of school in the eighth grade.

Robert Jones was eventually arrested at the age of 19 years old for crimes he did not commit. He was found guilty as an innocent man and was sentenced to serve life plus 121 years in Angola Louisiana State Penitentiary. While Robert was incarcerated he re-educated himself by obtaining his GED, learning the law, business, political science and a host of other subjects. He was also an inmate lawyer and organization leader amongst other prisoners.

After serving more than 23.5 years on a wrongful conviction, Robert is now a free man who has been cleared of all charges. He is a motivational speaker and a well-known community activist, poverty abolitionist and one of the co-founders of Free-Dem Foundations, Inc., a nonprofit organization that mentors and guides the youth in his community in a positive direction. Robert sits on the board of directors of two other nonprofit organizations and is on a city safety and justice advisory committee. He is currently starting his own businesses and employed as a client advocate with the Orleans Public Defenders Office.

Robert Jones is a co-author of the book, *Unbreakable Resolve: Triumphant Stories of Three True Gentlemen.*

Daniel Rideau is the second of five siblings born to Mrs. Deborah Rideau Gaines. Daniel spent his adolescent years in and out of juvenile facilities, which continued into early adulthood. At the age of 21 Daniel was sentenced to life in Angola State Penitentiary for murder, but later had his sentence reduced to manslaughter due to prosecution misconduct. Daniel was released in 2003, but arrested again in 2004 for identity theft and served five years in prison and five years on parole.

Daniel is a lifetime member of St. Luke Baptist Church where he sings in the choir and plays the drums. Daniel is a Master Barber and co-owner of Real Gentlemen Barbershop, LLC, and Co-Founder of Free-Dem Foundations, Inc.

His passion is to help disregarded youth find economical equality and self worth. Daniel is a co-author of *Unbreakable Resolve: Triumphant Stories of Three True Gentlemen.*

Daniel is a true gentleman.

"Know thyself. Own thyself."

Daniel Rideau

Jerome Morgan is a 40-year old true gentleman who was placed in foster care at the age of three and grew up in the neighborhood of Pontchartrain Park. At the age of 17 he was wrongfully imprisoned and sentenced to life without parole for a murder he did not commit. After 20 years spent in the Louisiana State Penitentiary, he bonded out and later had the charges "Nolle Passe" in May 2016 availing heavy re-prosecution.

Jerome Morgan Co-Founded Free-dem Foundations, Inc. He is a poverty expert, counselor and prisoner correspondent. He is a guest member of three churches: Christian Unity Baptist Church, St. Gabriel the Archangel Roman Catholic Church and New Life Ministry Baptist Church. Jerome advocates for the young people in his community at the Youth Empowerment Project, as a Social Justice co-facilitator in local schools, as a community activist with Students At the Center (SAC), Justice and Beyond, The New Jim Crow Ministries and Kid's Rethink New Orleans.

Jerome is a licensed barber at the business he co-owns: Real Gentlemen Barbershop, LLC (RGB). He is a graphic designer and writer with Park Roots Productions, LLC and a client of the Innocence Project New Orleans (IPNO). Jerome is a co-author of *Unbreakable Resolve: Triumphant Stories of Three True Gentlemen.*

Made in the USA
Coppell, TX
01 August 2020